LAW AND THE CONDITIONS OF FREEDOM

IN THE NINETEENTH-CENTURY UNITED STATES

LAW

AND THE CONDITIONS

OF FREEDOM

IN THE NINETEENTH-CENTURY

UNITED STATES

✦✦

JAMES WILLARD HURST

THE UNIVERSITY OF WISCONSIN PRESS

The University of Wisconsin Press
1930 Monroe Street
Madison, Wisconsin 53711

3 Henrietta Street
London WC2E 8LU, England

www.wisc.edu\wisconsinpress

4   6   8   9   7   5

Printed in the United States of America

Library of Congress Cataloging-in-Publication Data
Hurst, James Willard, 1910–
Law and the conditions of freedom in the
nineteenth-century United States.
Includes bibliographical references and index.
1. Law—United States—History and criticism.
2. Sociological jurisprudence.   I. Title.
KF366.H87   1986   349.73   56-9304
ISBN 0-299-01360-X   347.3
ISBN 0-299-01363-4 (pbk.)

FOREWORD

The Julius Rosenthal Foundation for General Law

THIS volume is the text of a series of lectures delivered under the auspices of the Julius Rosenthal Foundation at Northwestern University School of Law, in March, 1955.

Julius Rosenthal, an eminent and beloved member of the Chicago bar, was born in Germany on September 17, 1828. He pursued his studies at the Universities of Heidelberg and Freiburg, came to Chicago in July, 1854, and was admitted to the bar in 1860. He was especially prominent as a practitioner in the law of wills and in probate and real estate law. As librarian of the Chicago Law Institute from 1867 to 1877 and again from 1888 to 1903, and as its president from 1878 to 1880, he was chiefly responsible for its development. He was a member of the First Board of State Law Examiners of Illinois, and its secretary from 1897 to 1899. He died May 14, 1905.

Julius Rosenthal was a lawyer of great learning and rare scholarly attainments. He labored long and earnestly to establish the highest standards of legal scholarship. Throughout his career, his interest in the Northwestern University School of Law was constantly manifested.

To honor his memory the Julius Rosenthal Foundation for General Law was established in 1919 by his son, Lessing Rosenthal, his daughter, Mrs. George Pick, and Charles H. Hamill, Max Hart, Harry Hart, Mark Cresap, Frank M. Peters, Leo P. Wormser, F. Howard Eldridge, Willard L. King, Magnus Myres, Mrs. Joseph Schaffner, and Mrs. Otto L. Schmidt, all of Chicago, and the Honorable Julian W. Mack, of New York. Additional funds were provided under the will of Lessing Rosenthal, who died in 1949. The income derived from the Foundation is, among other uses, applicable to the cultivation of legal literature, and particularly to the publication of meritorious essays, monographs, and books of a scientific or practical nature concerning the law; to the aid or encouragement of research in the field of legal literature and the preparation for publication of the results of such research; and to the delivery and publication of lectures on subjects concerning the law.

v

ACKNOWLEDGMENT

THIS VOLUME owes its origin to an invitation to deliver the Rosenthal Foundation lectures at the Law School of Northwestern University. The essays report work in progress under a long-term program of research in the history of the interplay of law and other social institutions in the growth of the United States. I gratefully acknowledge the generous support given the whole project by the Rockefeller Foundation and, at an earlier stage, by the Social Science Research Council; my thanks go also for their continuing encouragement to Deans Lloyd K. Garrison, Oliver S. Rundell, and John Ritchie, and to my colleagues and to the President and Regents, of the University of Wisconsin. On this particular occasion my gratitude runs particularly to the law faculty of Northwestern University for the opportunity to present these lectures, and especially to Dean Harold C. Havighurst and Professors Brunson MacChesney and W. Willard Wirtz, for characteristic, warm hospitality. Of course, the essays do not purport to speak for any of these agencies or persons, and I take sole responsibility for what is said.

I am grateful for permissions received to quote from Dorfman, *The Economic Mind in American Civilization* (The Viking Press, Inc. New York, 1946); Goldmark, *Impatient Crusader* (The University of Illinois Press. Urbana, 1953); and Linton, *The Cultural Background of Personality* (Appleton-Century-Crofts, Inc. New York, 1945).

W. H.

CONTENTS

LAW AND THE CONDITIONS OF FREEDOM

IN THE NINETEENTH-CENTURY UNITED STATES

I

THE RELEASE OF ENERGY

ONE day in February of 1836, in the scarce-born village of Pike Creek on the southeastern Wisconsin shore of Lake Michigan, Jason Lothrop—Baptist minister, schoolteacher, boarding house proprietor, and civic leader—set up on a stump a rude press of his own construction and with ink which he had made himself printed a handbill setting forth the record of the organizational meeting of "The Pike River Claimants Union . . . for the attainment and security of titles to claims on Government lands."

The settlers whose Union this was had begun to move into the lands about Pike Creek beginning in the summer of 1835. They were squatters; put less sympathetically, they were trespassers. They might not lawfully come upon the lands before the federal survey was made, and this was not completed in this area until about February 1, 1836; they might not make formal entry and buy until the President proclaimed a sale day, and Presidents Jackson and Van Buren withheld proclaiming these newly surveyed lands until 1839; they might not establish claims by pre-emption, for the existing pre-emption law expired by limitation in June, 1836, and was not immediately renewed because of objections to speculators' abuses. These were formidable legal obstacles. The settlers' reaction tells us some basic things about the working legal philosophy of our nineteenth-century ancestors.

Jason Lothrop recalled twenty years later:

Much conflicting interest was manifest between the settlers, from the first, in making their claims. Some were greedy in securing at least one section of 640 acres for themselves, and some as much for all their friends whom they expected to settle in the country. Before the lands were surveyed, this often brought confusion and disputes with reference to boundary lines, and still greater confusion followed when the Government surveys were made in the winter of 1835–36. These contentions often led to bitter quarrels and even bloodshed.

The settlers met several times to discuss the need of a more orderly framework within which growth might go on. Finally their discussions pro-

3

duced a meeting at Bullen's store in Pike Creek on February 13, 1836, where they adopted the constitution of their Claimants Union. They created the office of Clerk and set the terms on which claims might be recorded with him, and they established a Board of Censors to adjudicate claims disputes. Through the turgid grandiloquence of their Constitution's preamble shows a pattern of attitudes and values which explains much about nineteenth-century law in the United States, reaching to concerns far greater than those of the tiny frontier village.

Whereas, a union and co-operation of all the inhabitants will be indispensably necessary, in case the pre-emption law should not pass, for the securing and protecting of our claims;

And whereas, we duly appreciate the benefit which may result from such an association, not only in regulating the manner of making and sustaining claims, and settling differences in regard to them, but in securing the same to the holders thereof against speculators at the land sale; and being well aware that consequences the most dangerous to the interests of settlers will follow, if such a union be not formed; and as Government has heretofore encouraged emigration by granting pre-emption to actual settlers, we are assured that our settling and cultivating the public lands is in accordance with the best wishes of Government; and knowing that in some instances our neighbors have been dealt with in an unfeeling manner, driven from their homes, their property destroyed, their persons attacked, and their lives jeopardized, to satisfy the malignant disposition of unprincipled and avaricious men; and looking upon such proceedings as unjust, calculated to produce anarchy, confusion and the like among us, destroy our fair prospects, subvert the good order of society, and render our homes the habitations of terror and distrust—those homes, to obtain which we left our friends, deprived ourselves of the many blessings and privileges of society, have borne the expenses, and encountered the hardships of a perilous journey, advancing into a space beyond the bounds of civilization, and having the many difficulties and obstructions of a state of nature to overcome, and on the peaceable possession of which our all is depending;

We, therefore, as well meaning inhabitants, having in view the promotion of the interest of our settlement, and knowing the many advantages derived from unity of feeling and action, do come forward this day, and solemnly pledge ourselves to render each other our mutual assistance, in the protection of our just rights. . . .[1]

Frontier communities have often been described as "lawless" or at least careless of law. It is too glib a characterization. True, the Pike Creek story was typical of many in the settlement of the Mississippi Valley. From the survey Ordinance of 1785 on, squatters settled large areas of the public lands in defiance of law, ahead of official survey, without color of title other than that created by the impact of a popular feeling that would not be denied. At government auctions, they assembled in force unlawfully to frighten off free outside bidding and prevent competition from forcing any of their company to pay the public land office more than the legal minimum to regularize his holdings. But, as at Pike Creek, while they waited for the public sale day, these settlers all over the central and midwestern states set up local governments in the form of "claims associations," elected officers with whom to record their land claims and from whom to obtain decisions of conflicts, and then generally abided among themselves by these records and decisions. Often unlawful in origin, settlement nevertheless quickly brought effective demand for law.

The preamble of the Pike Creek Claimants Union reflects in miniature two working principles by which we organized the relations of legal order and social order in the nineteenth-century United States. I speak particularly of "working" principles, principles defined and expressed primarily by action. It is in this aspect that the Pike Creek document is most relevant to our purpose. For these essays seek to understand the law not so much as it may appear to philosophers, but more as it had meaning for workaday people and was shaped by them to their wants and vision. Of course, this is not the only viewpoint from which to appraise the legal order. Nor is law that is formed largely by the imperatives of action necessarily the best law. We are simply trying one angle of vision provided by history for the distinctive reality it may disclose. Whatever its limitations, it is a point of view warranted by the central principle of our legal order, that law exists for the benefit of people and not people for the benefit of law. Such a legal order cannot in the long run be true to itself and at the same time be better than the values or vision of its beneficiaries. Moreover, emphasis on "working" principles seems peculiarly in point when we are trying to understand ourselves. Our history amply validates Tocqueville's observation that we have been a people not given to general theory; one usually senses that he is closer to apprehending the decisive faiths and beliefs of our nineteenth-century ancestors when he reads these out of what they did and said as they acted, rather than out of their self-conscious philosophizing.

The base lines of nineteenth-century public policy implicit in the Pike Creek document are three: (I) Human nature is creative, and its meaning lies largely in the expression of its creative capacity; hence it is socially desirable that there be broad opportunity for the release of creative human energy. (II) Corollary to the creative competence which characterizes human nature, the meaning of life for men rests also in their possessing liberty, which means basically possessing a wide practical range of options or choices as to what they do and how they are affected by circumstances. (III) These propositions have special significance for the future of mankind as they apply in the place and time of the adventure of the United States; here unclaimed natural abundance together with the promise of new technical command of nature dictate that men should realize their creative energy and exercise their liberty peculiarly in the realm of the economy to the enhancement of other human values.[2]

From these premises we drew two working principles concerning the uses of law. (1) The legal order should protect and promote the release of individual creative energy to the greatest extent compatible with the broad sharing of opportunity for such expression. In pursuit of this end, law might be used both (a) to secure a man a chance to be let alone, free of arbitrary public or private interference, while he showed what he could do, and (b) to provide instruments or procedures to lend the support of the organized community to the effecting of man's creative talents, even where this involved using the law's compulsion to enforce individual arrangements. (2) The legal order should mobilize the resources of the community to help shape an environment which would give men more liberty by increasing the practical range of choices open to them and minimizing the limiting force of circumstances. The people at Pike Creek wanted the community to guarantee their claims to be let alone in working their land and to lend its force to support their dealings with the land, that they might realize their "fair prospects." They also wanted the general government to use its resources positively to enlarge their opportunities as they sought to "overcome" "the many difficulties and obstructions of a state of nature"; to this end they wanted a preemption law or at least some affirmative legal preference of settlers over speculators.

Philosophers have expressed the ebullient force of western society by declaring that the end of law is to promote the maximum assertion of individual free will. This is too abstract talk to catch the policy flavor of our nineteenth-century statutes and court decisions. That policy looked toward very tangible ends and at the same time expressed a faith in human talent for creation and human need for creative expression which is not adequately conveyed by the philosophers' emphasis on "will."

However inadequately they expressed the vision, people in the nineteenth-century United States had already sighted the promise of a steeply rising curve of material productivity as the dynamic of a new kind of society. Some saw this dynamic mainly as a means to create new power and positions of leadership, and themselves as the men to take over these opportunities. Some visioned an enlarged, more self-respecting and creative life for great numbers of people, a higher ethic to be built paradoxically on material foundations. All had in common a deep faith in the social benefits to flow from a rapid increase in productivity; all shared an impatience to get on with the job by whatever means seemed functionally adapted to it, including the law.[3]

Impatient confidence in productivity, and hence in any positive or restrictive uses of law which would free more units of production, was natural to our situation. We came from a scarcity-conscious Old World into a rude new land where our own capital scarcity was a fact continuously weighing on us. We were the more dominated by the virtue of overcoming scarcity because the contrast between our limited resources and our vast opportunities constantly challenged and tantalized. Our prime inheritance was of middle-class ways of thinking. We continually experienced the tangible accomplishments of individuals, small groups, and local effort, with a heady sense of living in a fluid society in which all about him all the time one saw men moving to new positions of accomplishment and influence. Our background and experience in this country taught faith in the capacities of the productive talent residing in people. The obvious precept was to see that this energy was released for its maximum creative expression.

If one took at face value some judicial expositions of doctrines of "vested rights," or those economic propositions which Henry Carey set forth as axioms of nature, one might believe that law played a minimum positive role in shaping our nineteenth-century society. It has been common to label nineteenth-century legal policy as simple laissez faire, and political debate of the last sixty years has propagated a myth of a Golden Age in which our ancestors—sturdier than we—got along well enough if the legislature provided schools, the sheriff ran down horse thieves, the court tried farmers' title disputes, and otherwise the law left men to take care of themselves.

The record is different. Not the jealous limitation of the power of the state, but the release of individual creative energy was the dominant value. Where legal regulation or compulsion might promote the greater release of individual or group energies, we had no hesitancy in making affirmative use of law. Relative to the greater simplicity of structure in the Wisconsin community of 1836–1870, for example, there was hardly less readiness to use the positive power of the state than one sees in 1905–

1915 as we usher in the twentieth century of administrative regulation.

However, there is likely to be some basis in experience for every myth. The myth of our laissez faire past rests on two important aspects of our eighteenth- and nineteenth-century development: (1) the central place of the modern institution of private property in our politics as well as in our economic organization; (2) the extent to which the challenge of the unopened continent dominated our imagination until the last quarter of the last century.

Nineteenth-century preoccupation with the market as a key social institution led men to think of private property as an idea almost solely economic in its significance. But to the men whose bid for power formed the working institution of modern private property in the seventeenth and eighteenth centuries, property was chiefly a political idea. To them the heart of the matter was that law should define and guarantee a wider dispersion of the powers of decision in the community; this it did by committing to private hands legally protected control over the bulk of economic resources. Before the full tide of the disturbing forces we call the Commercial and Industrial Revolutions, power was tightly held in England. In various combinations at different times, it lay within a close circle of the Crown and its friends, the established church, the military, and the greater and lesser landed men. Commerce and industry put new means of influence into the hands of new men; these consolidated their opportunities by achieving a legal order which gave them large autonomy in commanding the economic resources on which their influence was founded.

Regarded thus as a political institution affecting the distribution of power, private property involved three central ideas in its English development, to which we added a fourth. (1) Since a high value was put on men's right to be let alone—to be "private"—there must be a reasonable public interest to justify imposing the public force on individuals' activities. This is the substance of what in the United States we eventually called "due process of law." (2) Such limits as government imposed on private freedom of decision must be declared according to a legitimate, public procedure, designed to keep law responsive to some influential nonofficial opinion. In our seventeenth-century inheritance this meant that an elected assembly should be the chief policy maker, its supremacy residing in its control of the public purse and its authority to ask questions about how the executive spent the public money. The original relation of this principle to the rise of the middle class was underlined by the property qualifications set upon the right to vote or hold legislative office, as well as by a traditional distrust of the executive as the historic source of arbitrary intrusions on privacy. (3) The legal order must provide every man with means to make formal insistence that law be applied to him fairly and impartially. Otherwise Crown grants of monopolies to court favorites or discriminatory taxes might soon make a sham of private freedom of action. In modern terms, there must be a guarantee of the equal protection of the laws for that framework of reasonable expectations within which alone private property would be meaningful. (4) Nineteenth-century United States legal growth added the elements of a judiciary given constitutionally guaranteed tenure during good behavior and authority to refuse effect to legislation found by the judges to be unconstitutional. Ready access to courts so armed added a factor that made itself deeply felt in our further definition of the property principle.[4]

These doctrines defined private property in terms of a legally assured measure of autonomy for private decision makers as against the public power. Of course, others than officials could threaten the security of private property; very old rules of criminal and tort law remind us that property is also the creation of the law's protection against the intrusions of arbitrary private force. But this latter role of the law was so taken for granted in early nineteenth-century policy as not to contribute much that is distinctive; as I have noted, despite easy generalizations about the "lawless" frontier, nothing is plainer than that settlement quickly brought demand for this kind of legal order. Some developments in nineteenth-century tort and criminal law promoted the release-of-energy policy. Otherwise, concern about the threat of private power to private property does not bring a fresh element into our legal history until the late-century interest in railroad and anti-trust regulation.

The order of events in time thus emphasized for the early nineteenth century the constitutional aspect of private property. In this context, property was primarily a bundle of legal limits on the intrusion of official power into nonofficial decision making; the seventeenth-century drama of conflict with the Crown had given a purely negative aspect to the institution.[5] However, there was nothing merely negative about the tone of life in the nineteenth-century United States. This obvious fact alone casts doubt on the adequacy of an exposition of nineteenth-century public policy which describes it solely in terms of negative propositions. We were a people going places in a hurry. Men in that frame of mind are not likely to be thinking only of the condition of their brakes. Thus, as we examine further we find that prevailing nineteenth-century attitudes in fact made private property pre-eminently a dynamic, not a static institution. Our situation was inappropriate to the growth of a dominant *rentier* interest, merely sitting on its possessions. We did not devote the prime energies of our legal growth to protecting those who sought the law's shelter simply for what they had; our enthusiasm ran rather to those who wanted the law's help positively to bring things about. The sign of this was the overwhelming predominance of the law of contract in all its ramifications in the legal growth of the first seventy-five years of the nineteenth century.[6]

The challenge of the unexploited continent was the second factor in disguising the actual extent of positive resort to law in shaping our society. This was what gripped our imagination and what has dominated our retrospect upon the century. The generally superficial and haphazard constitutional debates in the new states, the early established pattern of wholesale borrowing of statutes from older states, the fumbling, trial-and-error method by which new legislation evolved, all testify that we were conscious that we needed a legal framework, but were impatient of the time and effort it took to provide it. After the extraordinary generation of political activity that accompanied and followed the Revolution, for most of the nineteenth century we put little of our creative talent into making the basic framework of law except in areas which we saw most directly contributing to the release of private energy and the increase of private options. Politics in the grand sense had been the focus of our creative energy from 1765 to 1800, when first the impact of imperial policy and then the novelty of new governments forced us to attend to problems of the organization of power. With these matters apparently settled, and confronting the challenge of the continent, the nineteenth century was prepared to treat law more casually, as an instrument to be used wherever it looked as if it would be useful. This instrumentalist view tended to put aside consideration of the larger problems of the organization or limitation of power and to take for granted the law's framework-setting function to an extent that did not do justice to its actual importance.

Let us turn back to this central institution of private property. It consisted in very important degree of legal limitations on the power of government and so far seems to exalt laissez faire as the keystone policy. But the law of private property—the law of the autonomy of private decision makers—included also positive provision of legal procedures and tools and legal compulsions to create a framework of reasonable expectations within which rational decisions could be taken for the future.[7] Of course, businessmen's invention—and, even more, their initiative—joined that of lawyers to fashion instruments of dealing; and of course, men abide by their agreements for other reasons than fear of lawsuits. But it does not exaggerate the role of law to see that its procedures and compulsions were inextricably involved in the growth of our market economy. By providing authoritative forms of dealing and by enforcing valid agreements, we loaned the organized force of the community to private planners.

Throughout the enthusiastic nineteenth-century expansion of contract, two sobering strains of doctrine attested that the courts never wholly lost sight of the fact that their enforcement of promises involved delegating the public force in aid of private decision making. The first of these doctrines was that of consideration. Consideration has undoubtedly served various purposes, the origins and relative weight of which we still know remarkably little about. But, so far as its requirements induced deliberation in the parties, limited the law's support to seriously intended undertakings, or refused the law's aid to unconscionable coercion, the doctrine implicitly recognized that delegation of the public power was at stake and must be handled responsibly.[8] To the same effect was the caution with which courts held on to a residual authority to refuse to enforce agreements which they found to be against public policy. By enforcing a contract, the public power supported the decisions the agreement represented and so far inescapably shared moral responsibility for the social consequences. Mr. Chief Justice Dixon crisply summarized the point for the Wisconsin court: "The law will not aid in enforcing an unlawful contract. . . ." Another contract he found "to be illegal, corrupt, and contrary to the principles of public policy, and just such a contract as no court should sit in judgment upon, except to pronounce it void, and to dismiss any action brought to enforce it."[9] The United States Supreme Court put the issue in a twentieth-century context, in *Barrows* v. *Jackson*, when it ruled that a state court might not, consistent with the Fourteenth Amendment, entertain an action for damages for the vendee's breach of a covenant against conveyance of realty to a person "not wholly of the white or Caucasian race":

When . . . the parties cease to rely upon voluntary action to carry out the covenant and the State is asked to step in and give its sanction to the enforcement of the covenant, the first question that arises is whether a court's awarding damages constitutes state action under the Fourteenth Amendment. To compel respondent to respond in damages would be for the State to punish her for her failure to perform her covenant to continue to discriminate against non-

Caucasians in the use of her property. The result of that sanction by the State would be to encourage the use of restrictive covenants. To that extent, the State would act to put its sanction behind the covenants. If the State may thus punish respondent for her failure to carry out her covenant, she is coerced to continue to use her property in a discriminatory manner, which in essence is the purpose of the covenant. Thus, it becomes not respondent's voluntary choice but the State's choice that she observe her covenant or suffer damages.[10]

The limiting doctrine of consideration and the residual authority to refuse enforcement of agreements found to be against public policy were rare notes of caution amid a great nineteenth-century burst of social invention in contract. For a time the century seemed well satisfied to make the market its central institution, and contract set the legal framework for market dealing. A great expansion of legal procedures and instruments by which men might take decisions and set courses of action which the law would enforce expanded the power delegated to private hands. Thereby, also, the law greatly extended its reach into the organization of the economy.[11]

The nineteenth-century presumption always favored the exercise of the autonomy which the law of contract gave private decision makers. Thus, the restrictive features of the doctrine of consideration were offset by the general rule that, absent such gross inadequacy of consideration as to evidence fraud, mistake, or duress, the courts would not make the existence of a contract turn on the judges' appraisal of the worth of the exchange. So far as the illegality of agreements was concerned, the classic formulation by an English judge also expressed the working attitude of courts in the United States:

If there is one thing more than any other which public policy requires, it is that men of full age and competent understanding shall have the utmost liberty of contracting, and that contracts, when entered into freely and voluntarily, shall be held good and shall be enforced by courts of justice.[12]

The first and most dramatic victory of contract was its capture of the land. Though doctrines of primogeniture and entail were prominent in the land law of some colonies, the seventeenth-century beginnings of the recording act system expressed our early interest in turning land into a more readily transferable good. The sheer abundance of land was probably enough to assure that a static, feudal type of tenure could not take lasting root with us. We remember the one great Dutch patroonship and the several English "manors" of upper New York as oddities. Our southern plantation owners lacked the temper to make a feudal landed class; they were agricultural industrialists and miners of soil. Our northern farmers tended to be real estate speculators. Coming from a society where men typically expected to own and pass on to their sons land which they held in a long family line, Tocqueville was struck by his observation of the fact that

almost all the farmers of the United States combine some trade with agriculture; most of them make agriculture itself a trade. It seldom happens that an American farmer settles for good upon the land which he occupies; especially in the districts of the Far West, he brings land into tillage in order to sell it again, and not to farm it; he builds a farmhouse on the speculation that, as the state of the country will soon be changed by the increase of population, a good price may be obtained for it.[13]

Law thus ratified values early and deeply instilled in the behavior of the people, when in the years close after the Revolution we began to remove such feudal restrictions on alienation as we had suffered and to build up the intricate body of law concerning the recording acts and the title problems involved in the finance of land trading.[14] A leader in the debate on abolition of feudal land tenures in the New York State Constitutional Convention of 1846 spoke the dominant policy of the times. The step the Convention was discussing was one "involving a great principle of political economy, that was founded in right itself, and worthy of a place in the constitution. . . . [T]here should be no more restrictions placed upon the alienation of real estate than upon personal estate. Property was improved by passing from hand to hand. . . ."[15]

Responding to the needs of a growing commerce, the courts in the first half of the nineteenth century enlarged the array of procedures and instruments to promote dealing at a distance and on credit, and gave a contract emphasis to relations of employment, agency, and lease. The roots of this growth ran into the eighteenth century. But the bulk of the job was done after 1800; it understates the vigor and ingenuity of the work done to regard it simply as a consolidation of earlier beginnings. This was the outstanding area of common law development in the first half of the century, as judges exercised their invention in the law of negotiable instruments (notes, bills of exchange, bills of lading, warehouse receipts), of factors, of agency, of insurance, of banking.[16] Thinking did not yet run to extensive federal legislation in economic matters; state legislatures lacked experience and during a good number of decades were under a cloud; hence state and federal court judges did most of the work. The main area of legislative contribution, running through the century, was to elaborate liens and debtors' exemptions, relevant to the very important matter of the finance of small business, whether in trade, farming, building construction, or lumbering.[17]

Two lines of emphasis wove a varying pattern over the nineteenth century in this expansion of contract. On the one hand, the development of contract meant increasing the scope of individual discretion in the management of resources. This was especially marked in the first half of the century, as elements contributed by the parties' agreements were allowed to loom larger in situations where rights and duties once were almost wholly determined by relation. The terms of the contract, explicit or "implied," took on greater importance in shaping the relation of master and servant; leaseholds lost surviving vestiges of feudal incidents; the married women's property acts were a significant step in increasing the self-determining role of the wife in the household and outside. But the general extension of contract expressed, above all else, the increasing dominance of the market in social organization. As the market expanded, its functional needs tended toward greater emphasis on the regulatory rather than the individualizing aspect of contract law. Of course, all social living puts a premium on reasonable expectation and safe reliance on others' conduct; but the development of the market steadily increased the interlocking character of operations in this society and thus tended to raise men's need to be able to rely on one another's performance. Various features of our growing law of agreements reflected this. In more and more instances, from mid-century on, the law itself provided a framework for the parties' dealing, unless they explicitly contracted out of the transaction which the rules of law shaped for them. This was notably true in respect to the instruments of commerce—bills of lading, warehouse receipts, stock transfer documents—and the forms of association, especially the partnership or corporation. This development was a particularly important form of the more general, growing confidence of the courts in implying agreements from the parties' dealings and construing their agreements in the light of trade custom. An "objective" measure supplanted the test of "a meeting of minds" as the formula by which courts decided whether parties had made an agreement; as we shall note hereafter, this seems part of an effort broader than the field of contract law to provide people with more definite frames of reference for their ventures. Analogous efforts to supply some of the assurance which the market required may have been involved in doctrines of consideration which in effect required the parties to channel their transactions into recognized forms of dealing, and in judicial attempts to state rules of illusory simplicity, to determine the materiality of a failure in performance under an agreement. In the field of commercial transactions, especially, absolute concepts of property rights as a form of individual liberty yielded to doctrines intended to enforce the security of transactions. In all of these ways, contract law invoked the compulsive force of the state to set a framework for dealing, to an extent which must materially qualify appraisal of the laissez faire element in our policy.[18]

The creative area of contract law in the middle span of the century concerned the business corporation and its financial techniques. The corporation was the most potent single instrument which the law put at the disposal of private decision makers. In making it available, the law lent its weight to the thrust of ambitions which reshaped not only the business of the country but also its whole structure of power. Here the legislature played a larger role; indeed, it was largely the legislature's mistakes and misdeeds in regard to corporate business which damaged legislative standing in public opinion from about 1830 on. It was inevitable that the legislature play a larger part in regard to corporation law. It did not lie in judicial power to grant charters, and men saw issues in this field too broad and turbulent to fit within the confines of lawsuits.

The first issue was drawn between two different working ideas of what a corporation was. One saw it as a device of mercantilist policy, useful in great adventures for building the resources of the state. The other saw it as a convenient instrument of private enterprise. At the beginning of the nineteenth century we were still accustomed to thinking of the East India Company as the type of the corporation—a rare thing, an unusual grant of special privileges in law for purposes of high policy. At first, the facts of the situation were not such as to lead us much beyond this conception. Early business needs and capacities were too modest to generate much pressure for broad and routine resort to incorporation. Many nineteenth-century corporation charters justifiably took the form of "special" acts because they did in fact deal with special cases; government could not issue a charter for a central bank or for a major trunk line railroad—enterprises which would be felt through the length and breadth of a state and shape the whole future direction of its growth—as if no more were involved than chartering a clothespin manufacturer. Because so much was at stake, these special cases presented natural occasions for the spirited clash of interest groups and, directly or indirectly, furnished most of the well publicized instances of proved or suspected legislative corruption. These circumstances of cleavage and melodrama deeply colored popular attitudes toward the chartering of corporations, tending to confirm the East India Company stereotype. A corporation must inherently be a very unusual, and probably dangerously favored, creature when so much weighty controversy swirled about charters and the affairs of chartered companies. In this atmosphere of debate, it is not surprising that it took some time for men to begin to distinguish among kinds of corporations and to see that there was an emerging demand for a convenient business association, with affairs of limited impact on the community, far removed from high politics.

Thus the grant of corporate status became a notable issue in the years of Jacksonian Democracy. This did, indeed, involve serious issues concerning the power structure of the society; the Jacksonian polemics on this score forecast the issues in the background of the Granger movement and the Sherman Act. But, aside from the sensitive matter of banks, currency, and credit, the demand for freer incorporation, deep down, fitted the dominant temper of the times, Jacksonian as well as Whig. Hence the Jacksonians appear increasingly uncomfortable in their opposition. The special charters which fill so many bulky volumes of state session laws of 1830–1880 are on the whole disappointing to a searcher for melodrama or moral conflict. They tend soon to fall into patterns; quite evidently most of them answered to rather standard demands for the means of reaching rather standard business ends. Mostly their provisions deal with powers or privileges which strike a twentieth-century observer as commonplaces of modern business. The reader must scan their standardized clauses with a very careful eye if he would find the small variations which may represent the hidden grab or privilege which historical legend associates with the special charter era. When the special provisions are found, few are such as to give rise to any plausible suspicion that they represent sinister gain at the expense of public welfare. The more familiar one becomes with nineteenth-century special charters, the more he suspects that if there was corruption it likely took the form of charging unofficial toll for steering perfectly routine charters through the bustle of a session. Many special charters set limitations on corporate life, on landholdings of the corporation, and on its capital, to remind us of the contemporary distrust. Yet the charters are there on the books by the hundreds. That legislatures filled with turbulent debate over the privilege of incorporation nonetheless ground out special charters in quantity for fifty years indicates that some very basic policy of the times was being fulfilled. The later course of the public debate showed this; with considerable anticlimax, after the melodrama of earlier years, a main argument against continued special chartering came to be that it put an undue drain on the time of legislatures in meeting a standard and routine demand. Jacksonian Democracy reached its resolution of the matter by finding that the public interest was satisfied if the privilege of incorporation for ordinary business purposes was made available to all on equal terms.[19]

The substance of what business wanted from law was the provision for ordinary use of an organization through which entrepreneurs could better mobilize and release economic energy. Partly this business demand was to get rid of a limiting governmental policy; it sought release of the law's jealously restrictive control over this type of association. But it is characteristic of the nineteenth century that there was here also a demand for positive help from the law. Merely to be let alone to combine capital was not the substance of the entrepreneurs' desire. Here, as so often, a lively and pervasive sense of capital scarcity, relative to our opportunities, supplied the dynamic of public policy. One did not mobilize and discipline scattered resources merely by exhorting government to keep its hands off. Entrepreneurs wanted the positive prestige of the sanction of the state implicit in the charter grant. They wanted the aid of an orderly capital subscription procedure under which capital could be fed into the enterprise on a defined installment plan, with provisions for periodic assessments of stockholders and forfeitures to enforce assessments. The influence of provisions for the limited liability of corporate stockholders for the debts of the business has perhaps been exaggerated as a source of the pressure for incorporation. But, whatever the relative weight of this element, there is no doubt that the grant of the limited liability privilege was sought as a positive aid by law to the enlistment of capital. Entrepreneurs wanted, too, a form of organization which firmly and broadly delegated power over mobilized capital to managers and directors.

The last quarter of the nineteenth century made still clearer the fact that capital mobilization and discipline were the heart of the matter. For this, entrepreneurs wanted the law to provide them with a still more elaborate apparatus. Out of the ingenuity of lawyers and judges they got what they wanted in the development of the corporate trust indenture from the old real estate mortgage, in the fashioning of preferred and common stock, no par common stock, debentures, and auxiliary financing devices such as the equipment trust certificate.[20]

The years 1800–1875 were, then, above all else, the years of contract in our law. Behind this ebullient invention and expansion in contract were the restless spirit and hopeful ambition which struck Tocqueville as he looked at the United States in the 1830's. In such a society as this, he observed,

nothing is greater or more brilliant than commerce; it attracts the attention of the public and fills the imagination of the multitude; all energetic passions are directed towards it. . . . Those who live in the midst of democratic fluctuations have always before their eyes the image of chance; and they end by liking all undertakings in which chance plays a part. They are therefore all led to engage in commerce, not only for the sake of the profit it holds out to them, but for the love of the constant excitement occasioned by the pursuit. . . . In the United States the greatest undertakings and speculations are executed without difficulty, because the whole population are engaged in productive industry, and because the poorest as well as the most opulent members of the commonwealth are ready to combine their efforts for these purposes. . . . But what most astonishes me in the United States is not so much the marvelous grandeur of some undertakings as the innumerable multitude of small ones. . . .[21]

Central doctrines of the nineteenth-century law of crimes and tort offer another measure of the confident policy that lay behind the surge of invention in contract. Likewise, tort and criminal law show a mingling of limits put upon legal regulation and affirmative resort to law, as in the contract field, to promote the release of creative individual energy.

Proof of criminal intent—often, of a specific criminal intent—was the general requirement in the standard catalog of crimes in the first half of the century. This was so as to crimes against property or involving business dealings, in notable contrast to developments a hundred years later. Corollary to this, proof of reasonable mistake of fact would generally make out a defense. Of course, the requirement of a guilty mind as an essential to make out a crime had very old roots. Partly it responded to belief in the freedom of the human will and the consequent moral responsibility attending its exercise. But, also, the requirement was, as Mr. Justice Jackson observed, "as congenial to an intense individualism, and took deep and early root in American soil."[22]

The restrictive use of the intent element may best be seen where it is invoked on the shadowy borderline of criminality. Nineteenth-century judges, for example, showed a significant uneasiness when they confronted the vague contours of the crime of conspiracy, as that offense came down to them in Star Chamber precedent. One way to hold the expanding offense within definable bounds was to insist strictly on a showing of wrongful intention. A leading Pennsylvania opinion of 1821, by Justice Gibson, reflects the concern felt lest there be undue encroachment on freedom of action and decision:

When the crime [of conspiracy] became so far enlarged as to include cases where the act was not only lawful in the abstract, but also to be accomplished exclusively by the use of lawful means, it is obvious that distinctions as complicated and various as the relations and transactions of civil society, became instantly involved. . . . It will therefore be perceived that the motive for combining, or, what is the same thing, the nature of the object to be attained as a consequence of the lawful act is, in this class of cases, the discriminative circumstance. Where the act is lawful for an individual, it can be the subject of a conspiracy, when done in concert, only where there is a direct intention that injury shall result from it, or where the object is to benefit the conspirators to the prejudice of the public or the oppression of individuals, and where such prejudice or oppression is the natural and necessary consequence.[23]

The insistence on a showing of criminal intention amounted in effect to a presumption in favor of the independence of individual action. The middle-nineteenth-century rationale of the law of negligence, in tort, reflected the same basic value judgment. Expansion of economic energies brought men into closer, more continuous relations in situations increasingly likely to yield harm. Nonetheless, at first the law emphasized the social desirability of free individual action and decision. Liability in tort should normally rest on a showing of fault on the actor's part; action at one's peril was the exception. Hence the burden lay on the injured person to show reason why the law should intrude its force to shift some of the burden of loss onto the one who caused injury. "[T]he plaintiff must come prepared with evidence to show either that the intention was unlawful, or that the defendant was in fault," said Mr. Chief Justice Shaw in 1850, "for if the injury was unavoidable, and that the conduct of the defendant was free from blame, he will not be liable." [24] The exercise of ordinary care, moreover, justified the actor, though he did cause injury. For, said the Wisconsin court, "No person is required to exercise a greater degree of caution and prevision than is exercised by the mass of mankind. More care than that is usually impracticable. Ordinarily, the very highest degree of care possible will defeat the success of the enterprise. The law aims to be practical, and to favor what is practicable." [25]

The nineteenth-century law of damages expressed similar policy. It was socially desirable that men should take risks in the interest of production. The law should not lightly add risks of its own creation to those inherent in the business situation. This direction of policy was made explicit in an 1880 Wisconsin decision. A statute provided for enhanced damages against converters of timber; timber theft was a constant threat to the integrity of long-range investments in forest land, and the act plainly sought to give greater security to the long-term investor or speculator. But the Wisconsin court construed the statute strictly, so as not to allow the enhanced damages against a bona fide purchaser of stolen logs who had bought them for manufacturing purposes. The opinion shows a marked preference for dynamic as compared with static capital, as the court argues that

if such dealers [as the present defendant] are held responsible for every trespass committed by those who cut the logs purchased by them in good faith, and are subjected to the statutory rule of damages, no one could purchase logs, timber or lumber in the market with any safety. The result of such responsibility would necessarily be to embarrass and check an important business, and greatly to injure an important industry of the state.[26]

The risks involved in vague damages doctrine might burden business operation as much as the actual assessment of recoveries. Concern for market functioning thus pressed the courts toward more defined and limited damages rules. To encourage entrepreneurs by reducing risks, the English court in 1854 laid down what became the accepted rule, that damages for breach of contract should be limited to "such as may reasonably be supposed to have been in the contemplation of both parties, at the time they made the contract, as the probable result of the breach of it."[27] Tort cases evidenced a similar caution against creating indefinite risks of liability, especially during the rise of new industries in the first half of the century; for example, early difficulties of raising capital for railroads underlined the hazard of throttling promising beginnings by imposing too heavy financial burdens. Of course, it was also true that the functioning of a market-oriented, division-of-labor society rested on the maintenance of an assured framework of justifiable expectations as to other people's behavior. At some point, this emphasis was inconsistent with relieving entrepreneurs from damages liability. However, the extent of the inconsistency did not become clear until the enormous expansion of the use of machinery in the last quarter of the century.[28]

Characteristically, nineteenth-century criminal and tort law involved not only limitations in the interest of free private decision, but also positive regulations looking to that end. Criminal law extended its reach in the eighteenth and nineteenth centuries nowhere more conspicuously than in the law of theft. Growth of the law concerning embezzlement, theft by bailees, and the receipt of stolen goods went along with the expansion of the market economy; increased dealings at a distance, in reliance on others, and in volume created an impersonality of dealing which called for more intervention by law to secure the working minimum of reliable conduct.[29]

Nor was nineteenth-century tort law simply a collection of rules limiting liability for the consequences of private decision making. Where the courts believed that tort liability would contribute to the basic framework of reasonable expectations necessary to encourage men to venture and to rely on others for productive ends, the judges were prepared to see liability extended. A marked example was the growth and refinement of the law concerning a principal's liability in tort for acts of his agent. The principal's liability might contribute to the energies of an expanding market. For, said a South Carolina judge in 1841,

the principal is represented by the agent, and unless he is liable, the great operations of life cannot be carried on—no man would have adequate security for his person or his property. The owner of goods would not trust them on a railroad, or a steamboat, if his only security was the liability of the mere servants employed. No passenger would commit his safety to a railroad, steamboat or stage coach, if, in case of injury, he could look to none but the agents usually employed about these modes of transportation. So, also, no man would have any guarantee for the security of his property, if his only remedy for negligence was the irresponsible or insolvent agents which another might employ. . . .[30]

The emphasis in nineteenth-century criminal, tort, and contract law on "objective" measures of liability probably expressed in another form the regulatory use of law to promote the conditions for the release of energy. Whether a contract was made, or a crime committed, depended not on what men later claimed had been their "real" intention, but on what, in a court's estimation, a fair-minded person would at the time have taken to be their intention, measured by words and conduct and the consequences reasonably to be expected from them. In tort, a man would be held to the standard of the conduct of a reasonable and prudent man, and not to a measure tailored to his particular personality.

Concern for objectivity inheres in any system of official order where there is enough emphasis on generality and consistency to entitle the system to be called "law." Moreover, any legal system has its own administrative necessities, one category of which is shaped by the practical problems of proving matters of fact. There is no way in any case to prove a man's mental state except by some kind of external evidence; on the other hand, this necessary insistence on proof by overt event certainly does not mean that the law's often announced concern with intention is either fictitious or hypocritical.

Law emphasizes "objective" measures of liability, then, for reasons which have no peculiar relation to the particular circumstances of the nineteenth century. But it is also true that these objective measures had a special, functional importance in a society which made the market a key institution and a belief in the beneficence of released energy a prime article of faith. Such a society had a peculiar need to create and maintain a framework of reasonably well defined and assured expectations as to the likely official and nonofficial consequences of private venture and decision. Only within some minimum framework of reasonably predictable consequences were men likely to cultivate boldness and energy in action. Precedents for the objective measures of proof and standards of conduct in tort, crime, and contracts run back of the Commercial Revolution. But the clear-cut and substantial emphasis in this direction grows with the centuries of modern commerce and industry. Writing in 1855, Theophilus Parsons emphasized the framework function of law in a way distinctively characteristic of a market-oriented society:

The importance of a just and rational construction of every contract and every instrument, is obvious. But the importance of having this construction regulated by law, guided always by distinct principles, and in this way made uniform in practice, may not be so obvious, although we think it as certain and as great. If any one contract is properly construed, justice is done to the parties directly interested therein. But the rectitude, consistency, and uniformity of all construction enables all parties to do justice to themselves. For then all parties, before they enter into contracts, or make or accept instruments, may know the force and effect of the words they employ, of the precautions they use, and of the provisions which they make in their own behalf, or permit to be made by other parties.[31]

A restrictive, rather than affirmative, aspect of nineteenth-century law partly born of a similar desire to make more definite the framework of venture and expectation may be found in the history of statutory interpretation. The strict construction rules with which nineteenth-century cases abound probably derived from diverse policies. A desire to achieve greater certainty or definition of risks for men venturing property seems to have been one of them. Relieving a street railway company of a paving assessment by strict construction of the applicable statute, the Wisconsin court dogmatically asserted that "every statute which is in derogation of the right of property or that takes away the estate of the citizen, ought to be construed strictly. It should never be enlarged by an equitable construction." [32] Consistent with this approach, also, was its ruling that under an act making telegraph companies liable for "all damages" caused by failure of their agents in handling messages, the company was not to be held liable for mental distress damage. The common law rulings against allowance of such damages rested on the difficulty of estimating them and of holding recoveries within proper limits. ". . . [H]ad a radical change in the law relating to the kinds of suffering which should furnish a ground of damages been contemplated, the act would have expressed that intention in some unmistakable way." [33] So, too, the court would not liberally construe the coverage of a statute abolishing the fellow servant rule on "railroads":

It would be quite a stretch of construction for this court to hold that the heavy burdens of sec. 1816 were intended by the legislature to be imposed on electric interurban railways under the term "railroads," when the legislature could use and is accustomed to use the more specific description in legislation concerning the interurbans. Where a statute is drastic and its burdens heavy, it is not permissible to bring within its terms by latitudinarian construction those not named therein. This merely recognizes the intention which ordinarily accompanies any such command, and this principle lies at the basis of what is called strict construction.[34]

As the last case indicates, caution lest the uncertain scope of legal liability unduly add to the economic risks of business was one judicial reaction to the broadening current of economic regulatory laws in the late nineteenth century. This undertone of judicial policy continued into the twentieth century, to give continued life to the doctrine of strict construction of penal statutes, as we increasingly invoked criminal sanctions in economic regulation.[35]

We identify no legal development more sharply with the nineteenth century than the judicial protection of "vested rights." The modern concept of private property began with the tradition of the Parliamentary Revolution, involving reliance upon a legislative assembly responsive to propertied interests and armed with powers of purse and inquiry to curb the arbitrary intrusions of the executive. But legislatures in the United States did not rest on such well-defined and limited class interest as did the seventeenth- and eighteenth-century House of Commons. Soon repenting of the broad authority given the legislative branch in our earliest state constitutions, substantial interests pressed successfully for limitations written into constitutional form and supported the courts' authority to enforce the superiority of constitution over statute. A realistic understanding of the nineteenth century's faith in release of energy involves relating this to the vested rights doctrine.

"Vested rights" sounds like pure standpattism, as if it connoted merely protection of what is because it is, because nothing is valued more than stability. But on the whole, the nineteenth-century United States valued change more than stability and valued stability most often where it helped create a framework for change. The century so highly valued change because imagination could scarcely conceive that it could be other than for the better. We may look somewhat wryly on this faith, but we must acknowledge it as a prime fact in our nineteenth-century public policy making. Thus, the more one looks at the lines along which the vested rights doctrine grew, the less satisfied is he to appraise it as a simple expression in favor of the status quo. Dynamic rather than static property, property in motion or at risk rather than property secure and at rest, engaged our principal interest.

We were concerned with protecting private property chiefly for what it could do; as one looks at the facts of cases and pays somewhat less attention to the sonorous language of judicial opinions, he is impressed that what we did in the name of vested rights had less to do with protecting holdings than it had to do with protecting ventures. There is no key instance where vested rights doctrine protected a simple *rentier* interest. We abolished primogeniture and entail, disestablished the few established churches we had, and gave married women control of their property, all without serious barrier from vested rights doctrine. The Federal Constitution forbade the nation or the states to grant any title of nobility. The Northwest Ordinance and the consistent policy of Congress under its constitutional authority to admit new states together foreclosed development of a privileged Old State class by providing for entry of new states out of our western lands and fixing the policy that these be admitted on terms of political equality with the old. The bulk of the nineteenth-century cases which developed vested rights doctrine involved the conduct of business or capital venture, including land speculation. The later decisions which protected freedom of contract, or entrepreneurs' freedom, as a "liberty" guaranteed by the Fourteenth Amendment were only the most explicit indicators of the main current of our concern for vested rights. Looking back from a mid–twentieth-century United States characterized by steady expansion of one form or another of securities holdings among the upper middle class, one might see the Income Tax decision (1895) as an expression of *rentier* interest. But in its contemporary context the major significance of the decision was for large-scale capital formation and the shape of big business. The principal nineteenth-century vested rights cases which protect property simply as a claim to hold onto what one has are those concerning the valuation of property in eminent domain proceedings. Even these rest less on protection of vested rights as such than on a kind of insistence on equal protection of the laws, that a particular individual should not be made to bear out of his own resources the cost of a community benefit.[36]

Nineteenth-century vested rights doctrine developed chiefly in relation to protection of venture capital and the limited autonomy of business because through most of the century we were scarce of capital and of necessity were preoccupied with opening up the continent. We had neither the means nor the time for an important *rentier* class. Circumstances through the first three-quarters of the century thus never called for a major test of attitudes toward protecting the status quo simply as such, unless one counts the issue of slavery as an instance. No single neat formula can contain the whole of the tension between North and South or the whole of the moral problem presented by property in human beings. One element in northern support for confiscating the property in slaves was the conviction that slavery had proved to be a system which did not fulfill the proper property function of generating a constantly expanding reach of human creative power. Nor should we forget that Lincoln drew the ultimate issue as the preservation of Union, whether any particular form of private property stood or fell.[37]

Of course, there were decisions, and there was much judicial language, looking to the protection of property considered simply as a claim to the maintenance of what someone had or the situation he was in. But it is important to note that the main current ran to the protection of property in action, for otherwise we may be surprised by some of the limits the nineteenth century put on protection of vested rights. A Wisconsin Supreme Court opinion of 1860 expresses the period's central concern with the safeguarding of venture capital. Asked to overrule an 1849 decision which had sustained the constitutionality of the mill-dam act, the court refused, though it indicated that as an original matter it would not now sanction the statute, which in effect delegated the power of eminent domain to waterpower developers who wished to flow others' land. Since the 1849 case, said Justice Cole, it was fair to assume that large amounts of capital had been invested in reliance on it.

And, although the period has been comparatively brief since the [1849] case . . . was decided, yet we all know that within that time enterprising towns and flourishing villages have grown up, whose wealth and prosperity are mainly dependent upon their hydraulic power, and whose business relations and industrial resources would be seriously affected, if we were now to overrule that case. . . . The rule *stare decisis,* has great force in such a state of things, and emphatically applies.[38]

Because it most valued private property for its productive potential, the nineteenth century was prepared to make strong, positive use of law to maintain such conditions as it thought essential to the main flow of private activity. Bankruptcy law began mainly as a protection to creditors against the dishonesty of debtors. But by mid–nineteenth century, both in national bankruptcy laws and in state insolvency legislation, the trend of policy was as much to provide means by which debtors might be saved from irretrievable ruin and salvaged as venturers who might yet again contribute productively to the market. "The discharge of the debtor has come to be an object of no less concern than the distribution of his property" under federal bankruptcy policy.[39] The contract clause of the Federal Constitution prevented state insolvency laws from discharging debts contracted before their enactment. But no contract clause limited the Federal bankruptcy power. The Fifth Amendment might bar destruction of a creditor's security interest in specific property acquired before passage of a bankruptcy law, but there was no taking of property without due process of law in employing a bankruptcy act to discharge debts contracted before the law went on the books.

In no just sense do such governmental regulations deprive a person of his property without due process of law. They simply require each individual to so conduct himself for the general good as not unnecessarily to injure another. . . . Every member of a political community must necessarily part with some of the rights which, as an individual, not affected by his relation to others, he might have retained. Such concessions make up the consideration he gives for the obligation of the body politic to protect him in life, liberty, and property. Bankrupt laws, whatever may be the form they assume, are of that character.[40]

Likewise valid, if they were not too drastic, were laws which stayed a creditor's remedies to afford the debtor a breathing spell in which he might regather his strength. Again, a test was whether the regulation would tend reasonably to preserve the general course of dealing. Mr. Chief Justice Dixon put it so for the Wisconsin court in sustaining an 1858 statute extending the time in foreclosures:

Although such changes are in general exceedingly unwise and unjust, yet if from sudden and unlooked-for reverses or misfortune, or any other cause, the existing remedies become so stringent in all or a particular class of actions that great and extensive sacrifices of property will ensue, without benefit to the creditor or relief to the debtor, a relaxation of the remedies becomes a positive duty which the State owes to its citizens.[41]

Of broader but analogous policy import were other familiar nineteenth-century rulings that vested rights must yield before government action to maintain the general framework of dealings. The community might take for a public highway a bridge owned by a private corporation under a legislative franchise given long before the applicable eminent domain statute was passed; here was no impairment of the obligation of contract, for every contract is made subject to exercise of the frame-work-setting powers of government.[42] Likewise the contracts clause was held not to limit the general power to tax or the police power.[43] Most drastic in application to existing commitments and expectations was the holding that Congress might provide for the issue of paper money and make it legal tender for debts previously incurred.[44]

It was natural to its buoyant optimism and its confidence in the re-lease of energy that nineteenth-century law coupled concern for vested rights with a high regard for keeping open the channels of change. This was one aspect of the bankruptcy and insolvency laws. It is a viewpoint implicit in the type of decisions just noted, in which judges were alert to protect the community's authority to deal with shifting conditions affecting the functional integrity of the whole system. The classic state-ment of policy in favor of freedom for creative change as against un-yielding protection for existing commitments was Taney's opinion in the *Charles River Bridge* case. Public grants should be strictly con-strued in favor of the public; nothing should pass by implication; hence the legislative grant of a franchise to build and operate a toll bridge should not be held by implication to give the grantees an exclusive charter, so that they might prevent the building of a nearby competing bridge under a later grant.

. . . [I]n a country like ours, free, active, and enterprising, continually advanc-ing in numbers and wealth, new channels of communication are daily found necessary, both for travel and trade; and are essential to the comfort, convenience, and prosperity of the people. A State ought never to be presumed to surrender this power [of promoting the happiness and prosperity of the community], because, like the taxing power, the whole community have an interest in preserving it undiminished. . . . No one will question that the interests of the great body of the people of the State, would, in this instance, be affected by the surrender of this great line of travel to a single corporation, with the right to exact toll, and exclude competition for seventy years. While the rights of private property are sacredly guarded, we must not forget that the community also have rights, and that the happiness and well being of every citizen depends on their faithful preservation.

The preference for dynamic rather than static property, or for property put to creative new use rather than property content with what it is, emerges in Taney's further description of the policy choices implicit in the case:

If this court should establish the principles now contended for, what is to become of the numerous railroads established on the same line of travel with turnpike companies; and which have rendered the franchises of the turnpike corporations of no value? Let it once be understood that such charters carry with them these implied contracts, and give this unknown and undefined property in a line of travelling, and you will soon find the old turnpike corporations awakening from their sleep, and calling upon this court to put down the improvements which have taken their place. The millions of property which have been invested in railroads and canals, upon lines of travel which had been before occupied by turnpike corporations, will be put in jeopardy. We shall be thrown back to the improvements of the last century, and obliged to stand still, until the claims of the old turnpike corporations shall be satisfied, and they shall consent to permit these States to avail themselves of the lights of modern science, and to partake of the benefit of those improvements which are now adding to the wealth and prosperity, and the convenience and comfort of every other part of the civilized world.[45]

The uniform legislative reaction to the *Dartmouth College* case made it clear that Taney expressed the dominant mid-century preference for property as an institution of growth rather than merely of security. With little question or exception, in the very act of providing franchises for private capital development, state constitution makers and legislators developed the practice of including in their grants a standard reservation of legislative authority to amend or repeal what they gave. Governors' vetoes, enforcing this policy, made explicit its preference for retaining maneuverability in the face of an always evolving situation. Thus, in 1882 Wisconsin's Governor Rusk vetoed a dam franchise given to named individuals because the statute did not include a reserved power of repeal or amendment analogous to the reservation which the state constitution made as to all grants to corporations. His message mingles characteristic policy tones of the century: law must provide a framework within which many may venture, rather than a favored few, and it must take care that future release of creative energy is not barred by the rigidity of old concessions:

The improvement may be for the public good, the tolls fixed may be fair and reasonable, but nearly all such measures affect the interests of many who know nothing of their pendency and are unheard as to their effect. In the nature of things it is impracticable for the legislature to make thorough and exhaustive investigation in each case, and to know the precise effect upon all interests of the measures asked for. Moreover, what may be an improvement in the situation of affairs to-day, may be very far from an improvement a few years hence; and what may be fair compensation for maintaining dams and other public improvements to-day, may not be fair or reasonable after the lapse of time. So that the public interest would seem seriously to demand that the legislature in all such grants should reserve to itself the right, should the public interest require it, to revoke the same, or to continue them upon new terms and subject to additional restrictions.[46]

To this point, I have sketched the release-of-energy policy almost entirely in terms of the relation of law to the economy. This accords with the emphasis which the times gave this policy. It was a century which put all the energy and attention it could into economic interests. Politicians might concern themselves with the sectional balance of power and humanitarians with slavery and drink and the rights of women. From time to time the zealous minority interested in these matters could whip up a general, emotional reaction to them. But in most affairs one senses that men turned to noneconomic issues grudgingly or as a form of diversion and excitement or in spurts of bad conscience over neglected problems. The law of the first half of the century particularly reflects this; in the latter half, simple social mechanics, the force of stubborn facts, began to bring law into contact with a wider range of concerns than those immediately economic.

General policy, expressed in practice more often than in formal declaration, favored the release of individual creativity in areas of life apart from the market. But the law played a quite indirect role in this. So far as colonial laws set limits on men's freedom to choose their religion or to gather with their fellows in sociable groups or to set their personal patterns of expenditure and their personal choices of pleasure, these were largely repealed or fallen into disuse amounting to practical repeal by the end of the first quarter of the nineteenth century. Where there was formal legal action to remove old limitations, as in the disestablishment of churches, it is difficult to believe that law brought about the change, rather than ratifying changes produced by social facts —by our fluid class structure, our abundance of land, our growing population with its recurrent waves of immigration.

The most important nineteenth-century uses of law in relation to social problems involved the control of the general environment. So far as concerns the simple release of individual energy in social affairs, law had its principal influence in the tolerance, protection, sometimes fostering, of associations of all kinds. Legally assured freedom of religious association was in the background of one of the most dynamic elements of the first half of the century: the evangelical Protestant movement in the rural areas, especially on the frontier, whose credo of individual dignity generated much of the emotional fervor of agrarian politics. Freedom of association let loose another dynamic factor for individualism in the Abolitionist societies. Liquor control became a fighting issue because there could be temperance societies; liquor and suffrage both came into the arena because women could organize groups on such public issues before they were able to vote or to manage property. Outside of the economic area religion was involved in the most serious conflicts over free association, in controversies over Masonic lodges, Catholic convents and schools, and Mormon communities. These figured in local and national politics in rather sporadic bursts of attention. Some legislation went on the books regulating secret societies; some additions were made to that pragmatic store of precedents which constitutes our policy of "separation of church and state"; some serious violence reminded us that effective civil liberty requires the positive protection of law. In the first half of the century these matters have significance primarily as parts of our history of middle-class morals and values, and of population growth and immigration; they involve legal history only indirectly.[47]

Freedom in political activity expressed a number of important public policies, besides promoting release of the individual's creative energies. Political participation is relevant to social interest in human dignity, in the legitimacy and distribution of power, and in the simple administrative necessity of getting questions settled. But, among these other objectives, a continuing inheritance from Jefferson was the faith that broad popular political activity would multiply fruitful thought, insight, invention in public affairs, to the general benefit.

The removal of property qualifications on voting or holding office was the outstanding action in law to set free men's political energies. The current set firmly in this direction as early as the New York constitutional convention of 1821, where the aged Kent futilely opposed it. In the newer states white male suffrage was not a serious issue, but the vote for free Negroes, for immigrants, and for women stirred controversies throughout the century. Emancipation of the slaves brought problems which called for positive implementation in law, if political freedom were to be real, and which remained as unresolved civil liberties issues of the nineteenth century.

Political freedom for individuals involves other civil liberties besides the right to vote: rights of free speech, press, assembly and petition, and of access to and enjoyment of the proper procedures of the civilian courts. The Alien and Sedition Acts, the Civil War and Reconstruction, and the conflicts over labor organization late in the century produced the notable problems on these fronts. The enforced lapse of the Alien and Sedition Acts was the clearest substantial victory of the century for the release-of-energy principle in these fields. The great civil liberties decision arising out of the Civil War—*Ex parte Milligan*—came after the crisis that produced the issue had abated. The transfer of political leadership from Radical Republicans to men whose prime interest was in economic growth, and the acquiescence of the Supreme Court in this direction of policy, ended for the nineteenth century any aggressive program in law to implement the liberty granted the Negroes in the South. No firm precedent for individual liberty emerged from the labor difficulties of the end of the century except so far as Altgeld's courageous pardon of the Haymarket anarchists admonished of the fundamental importance of a fair and temperate trial process. More typical of the indecisiveness of the law's role in civil liberties in these years was the flamboyant resurrection of an obsolete theory of "treason" to indict leaders of the Homestead strike, followed after a time by quiet dropping of the charges.[48]

The nineteenth century produced some important issues for individual civil liberties, but showed no impressive record of grappling with them. It is symbolic that the most decisive episode, the controversy leading to the nonrenewal of the Alien and Sedition Acts, came at the opening of the century, in our classic generation of high politics. There is little that happens after 1800, until the Holmes-Brandeis dissents begin to build a supporting body of opinion in the 1920's, to suggest the presence of a really substantial public opinion interested in and prepared to pay the costs of supporting individual civil liberties. It would distort the view of our nineteenth-century life to say that it embodied any substantial, defined hostility to individual political freedoms; the accepted and revered political generalities all exalted individual liberty. But the century was so market-focused as to be politically naive. Its prevailing attitudes tended to range from indifference to impatience with matters that distracted attention from "progress," defined as increase of capital and consumable wealth. Toward the end of the century the right of association took on high importance in practice, but this was felt then more as a matter of redressing the general balance of power in the society than as an issue of individualism. All this is part of our inheritance, along with the Bill of Rights. One could not be certain how different was the alignment of working belief on the value of individual civil liberty in the mid–twentieth century, except that in the later time we were more impatient with what distracted from attention to "security" than we were with interruptions to "progress." At least in the 1950's, however, the weight to be placed on individual civil liberties was recognized as a major political issue; in that respect, the situation stood in marked contrast to that of most of the nineteenth century.

Belief in the release of private individual and group energies thus furnished one of the working principles which give the coherence of character to our early nineteenth-century public policy. This principle found expression in no simple removal of legal restrictions or staying of the regulatory hand. Limitations on official power were very important elements of this pattern of policy. But so, too, was a complicated affirmative use of law to furnish instruments and procedures and to impose as well as enforce patterns of dealing. In this aspect, our nineteenth-century policy involved a good deal less of simple laissez faire than has often been claimed for it. Joseph Spengler has properly cautioned against exaggerating the extent of legal intervention in the economy by way of regulatory laws: such government operations tend to leave a larger residue of records, especially in comparison with the relatively simple, nonbureaucratized business of the early part of the century; moreover, in their nature such intervention and the advocacy of such intervention are more likely to leave positive records of initiatives taken or proposed than is the advocacy of a negative position.[49] It is true, however, as Chapter Two will note, that we made considerable use of legal compulsion to meet the challenge of our environment and that by no means did we always treat the release of energy as wholly beneficent. When these regulatory uses of law are taken together with the framework of legal compulsion within which the regime of contract operated, it is plain that while the enlargement of men's freedom was the objective, it was, indeed, freedom under law.

II

THE CONTROL OF ENVIRONMENT

W E were all Republicans, we were all Federalists, in possessing a common instrumental belief which shaped the nineteenth-century legal order. Jefferson and Hamilton, Jacksonian and Whig, were alike confident that men could materially control their environment through the legally mobilized power of the community. George Bancroft spoke in 1835 with the gusty exuberance and vague idealism of Jacksonian Democracy. But he expressed the general view of man's peculiar capacity to change things:

The material world does not change in its masses or in its powers. The stars shine with no more lustre than when they first sang together in the glory of their birth. . . . Nature is the same. For her no new forces are generated; no new capacities are discovered. The earth turns on its axis, and perfects its revolutions, and renews its seasons, without increase or advancement. But a like passive destiny does not attach to the inhabitants of the earth. For them the expectations of social improvement are no delusion; the hopes of philanthropy are more than a dream.[1]

Such faith in our capacity to affect the currents of events was implicit in Jefferson's program to use the public lands to center American society around the small farmer, and his plans for a public schools system (indeed, also, in the Louisiana Purchase); in Hamilton's proposal of a protective tariff to promote industry; in Clay's argument for a bold public scheme of internal improvements.

Thus, Jefferson saw public education as a force which might fundamentally mould the society. The public schools would both develop human resources and create the conditions of a proper internal balance of power:

By that part of our plan which prescribes the selection of the youths of genius from among the classes of the poor, we hope to avail the State of those talents which nature has sown as liberally among the poor as the rich, but which perish without use, if not sought for and cultivated. But of the views of this law none is more important, none more legitimate, than that

33

of rendering the people the safe, as they are the ultimate, guardians of their own liberty. . . . Every government degenerates when trusted to the rulers of the people alone. The people themselves therefore are its only safe depositories. And to render even them safe, their minds must be improved to a certain degree. This indeed is not all that is necessary, though it be essentially necessary. An amendment of our constitution must here come in aid of the public education. The influence over government must be shared among all the people. . . .[2]

Hamilton and Clay viewed the economy as a field of energy in which government could supply important direction. Would not industry develop without governmental aid as fast as the facts and the public interest required? Hamilton argued that there were "very cogent reasons" for believing the contrary:

These have relation to the strong influence of habit and the spirit of imitation; the fear of want of success in untried enterprises; the intrinsic difficulties incident to the first essays toward a competition with those who have previously attained to perfection in the business to be attempted; the bounties, premiums and other artificial encouragements with which foreign nations second the exertions of their own citizens, in the branches in which they are to be rivaled. . . .[3]

The importance of the commerce power of the central government, urged Clay, was its positive character; it should be used affirmatively, both for economic growth and political stability.

The power to regulate commerce among the several states, if it has any meaning, implies authority to foster it, to promote it, to bestow on it facilities similar to those which have been conceded to our foreign trade. . . . All the powers of this government should be interpreted in reference to its first, its best, its greatest object, the union of these states. And is not that union best invigorated by an intimate, social, and commercial connexion between all parts of the confederacy? Can that be accomplished, that is, can the federative objects of this government be attained, but by the application of federative resources? [4]

Our place and time in history made it natural that we should confront the challenges of our environment with increasing confidence that we could master circumstance. Experience taught us so, and social inheritance made us receptive to the lesson.

The setting dramatized the issue between man and environment. Most obvious was the challenge of physical fact; for 250 years as we drove inland from our coasts, again and again we had to master wilderness and distance. The social setting highlighted our opportunity to fashion the environment of community. We confronted no elaborate, deepset pattern of Indian institutions which we must overcome or assimilate, unless one counts the influence of frontier warfare upon our security measures. In this context, even to borrow English institutions subtly taught us that we could contrive a society from a standing start. During 150 years of colonialism geographical remoteness and the problems of finding markets hammered at us that we must rely on our devising.

Nineteenth-century public land policy evidences attitudes we learned from challenging the wilderness and writing our social rules on a relatively clean slate. Particularly, we learned to regard settlement as unquestionably a value in itself; government was under constant, almost invariably successful pressure to bring land to market and, less successfully, to adopt policies which would put it immediately into the hands of small cultivators. Characteristically, in 1849 Wisconsin's first governor made this a major issue of his first message to the legislature:

The present manner of disposing of the national domain in unlimited quantities has become a striking evil. In many parts of our State, individuals, and some are not even citizens or residents of the United States, have purchased large quantities of the best lands, and the settlement of the country has been thereby greatly retarded. Settlers have been compelled to pay an advanced price for their homes, and to increase by their labor the value of the wild land of non-residents, without any corresponding benefit to the holders, and the investment in many cases is unprofitable.[5]

The limitations on state participation in works of internal improvement, which became standard in constitutions following the incautious canal and railroad subsidies of mid-century, bore witness to one spectacular expression of our bold readiness to shape the physical environment to the social. The luxuriant growth of the law of eminent domain in the nineteenth-century United States likewise attested the freedom with which we indulged in social invention against the challenge of nature.[6]

Our location in time also bred confidence that we could shape things and relations to our purpose. It was of definitive importance in our legal history that the firm settlement of the North American continent came in the seventeenth and eighteenth centuries rather than in the fourteenth, and by people whose lives were already caught up in the Commercial Revolution. North American growth was thus early and inseparably part of the expansion of middle-class energy, which here found its most distinctive expression. The tone of this society was set by men for whom life's meaning lay in striving, creation, change, and mobility.

The timing of our settlement was important, also, because it fell at the opening of a great acceleration in the pace, range, and depth of social change. True, simplicity enforced by scarcity held social and economic change to a slow march through many of the years before 1800. But nationalism and scientific, technical, and market invention had loosed currents which ran too hard not to cause disturbance somewhere in any society they touched. We first acutely felt this unsettlement in politics; as the home country pressed for imperial profits, the colonists became increasingly preoccupied with issues of the organization of political power. While we moved into the nineteenth century, technological and market invention set a higher tempo of change on a broader front and with insistent recurrence jolted men out of the notion that conditions and ways of life were fixed; it became the common experience that a man lived his mature years in a social environment radically different from that of his youth. Whatever the mixture of illusion with reality, our experience of change, evaluated from a middle-class view of life, taught us to think that we moved events. In our classic period of politics, our preoccupation, significantly, was with making constitutions—legal frameworks for growth. As we turned to an economic focus, the release-of-energy principle, with its predominant outlet in contract, expressed our middle-class confidence in contriving. Amid the "vested rights" decisions prominent in mid-century legal development, one finds also sturdy assertion that the community may legitimately intervene to reshape a disadvantageous drift of events by exercising that "police power of the State [which] extends to the protection of the lives, limbs, health, comfort, and quiet of all persons, and the protection of all property within the State," and which leaves it "within the range of legislative action to define the mode and manner in which every one may so use his own as not to injure others." [7]

However, this takes us only one step. To believe that men can command environment is one thing; to determine for what ends they shall use their mastery is another. Thus, as men increase their command of environment, they increase freedom of choice; but in itself this does not tell us whose freedom is enlarged. The history of public policy written into law takes on distinctive character for different periods depending on the answer to this last question. In this country the nineteenth-century legal order emphasized individualism, in contrast to a sharper eighteenth-century concern for the integrity of the community. To the nineteenth century liberty meant liberty for individuals.

The nineteenth century saw two aspects to the achievement of liberty. (1) Partly it saw liberty in the release of men's innate capacities: they should be let alone to show what they could do. This was an inheritance from the Renaissance, from Tudor England, with roots deep in traditions of classic Athens and the Roman Republic. One senses this Renaissance quality in the bursting vitality of contract invention. (2) But men also experience liberty as the possession of options, of practical power to say something about what they do and what happens to them. If some find freedom of will an illusion, yet plainly an everyday belief in it materially influenced our legal history. To think of liberty as possession of a range of options quickly brings one up against rude facts of environment and soon brings demands upon the positive power of the state. Liberty as simple release of energy is the liberty guaranteed by the negatives which the Bill of Rights sets on official power. Liberty as enlargement of options is the liberty we know as created by laws which secure public health, education, the market, and peaceable political processes.

The individualism of nineteenth-century law drew on values rooted in our colonial past. But there was a difference and tension between social-economic and legal growth in the colonial years. Social and economic development tended to create a way of life and a pattern of human relations which generated in individuals habits of independence and expectations of mobility in social status or influence. But through a good part of the colonial years the dominant tone in the law was defensive rather than expansive, favoring stability rather than change and emphasizing the security or strength of the colony more than the freedom of the individual. So far as we used law to meet the challenge of environment, colonial statute books imply that we sought primarily to enlarge the range of options of the community as a social entity.

Security was a natural emphasis in colonial law. Isolated, endangered by Indians and imperial rivalries, we felt the need to draw tightly together in our separate colonies. We had to build an economy out of little capital and limited manpower and skills; it was important to all that work be done and be adequate, that goods be marketable, that internal tensions be carefully watched, when the society as a whole lived on a narrow margin between safety and peril, a good living and mere subsistence.

Overriding concern for community security had political expression in loyalty legislation. With marked uniformity, the colonies legislated against treason, trade with enemies, and espionage in sweeping terms which favored the state and cast the doubt against the individual. It was a tone quite different from that taken by the men who later wrote into the Federal Constitution a cautiously restricted treason clause and a Bill of Rights. Laws compelling attendance at church, forbidding secular intrusions on the Sabbath, restricting luxury expenditures on food, drink, and clothing, limiting wages and restricting the alienation of land were the social expression of the early colonial drive for security by law. On their face, many such regulations were concerned with men's souls, or at least their morals. But in the background was the consciousness of lonely communities on trial before God and the hard facts. There was all too little strength to meet the challenge of our situation; we must hold closely together, save and not waste, and prevent internal dissensions born of envy and unseemly striving. Finally, the seventeenth- and eighteenth-century colonial statutes were full of economic regulations which declared a mercantilist conviction that a colony must find strength as an ordered community. How men did their jobs was important to the general life; regulations of "common callings" stretched beyond the later notion of the "public utility." The community's welfare was intimately involved with the reception of its exports in strange markets; hence the law set standards of quality and measure, provided close inspection, and put the public seal on cask or barrel, that the stamp of official approval might give the goods greater currency. The margin was narrow between good times and hard times; there was sharp worry lest faulty market functioning impede production; hence there were regulations of price and marketing practices.[8]

The years of the Revolution present a rather confusing crisscross of policy currents. The division of Tory and Patriot brought a stiffening of loyalty legislation, notably in the confiscation of Tory property. On the other hand, these years began the relaxation of social regulations affecting class or status, especially by abolition of feudal land tenures and extension of the suffrage. But the new state constitutions conferred practically unlimited power on the legislatures, and this was exercised in an important range of economic regulation, including price fixing, control of trade practices, and limiting of creditors' rights. Not until after the later period of constitution making, starting with the more conservative Massachusetts Constitution of 1780 and ending with the adoption of the Federal Constitution, did the statute books reflect a new direction of emphasis. Thenceforth, community security was taken for granted; when we resorted to law to shape the conditions of life, it was more and more to enlarge the range of options open to private individuals and groups.

All of the legal means for shaping environment rest on that possession of the legitimate monopoly of force which is a distinctive mark of law. But this force may be exerted more or less indirectly. In the nineteenth century we used law to shape environment (1) by directing or affecting the allocation of economic resources, (2) by regulating behavior, (3) by affecting, and in a small degree directing, the advancement of knowledge or belief and the formation of public opinion in consequence. The second and third approaches always involved some legal allocation of resources (by legislative appropriations to executive agencies, or direct or indirect public subsidy to nonofficial agencies), but in relation to total community resources the allocations were too small to count in themselves as a significant form of legal intervention. The allocation of resources might be a very powerful form of regulation of behavior; it is singled out because it was used in such particular fields and involved such particular problems of policy as to have its own character. Promotion of knowledge or belief may likewise be a powerful form of regulation of conduct, though by indirection; it is singled out because it has its own period of development, with limited nineteenth-century beginnings whose main interest is for what they foreshadow of twentieth-century problems.

It also helps in seeking pattern in a turbulently confused nineteenth century to note that men faced the challenge of three environments. Most obvious was that presented by nature apart from man. Equally imperative, however, were the conditions of social living, the social environment, without which man is only another animal. Subtlest and the last to be envisaged as presenting a challenge was the individual's internal environment, formed by the pattern of deepset emotional drives and the values resting thereon, within whose frame reason must operate.

Nineteenth-century policy moved in successive waves of response, now to one felt challenge of environment, now to another. Constant in the background, however, was the theme of resort to law to enlarge the options open to private individual and group energy. This was a basic point of contrast with the seventeenth- and early eighteenth-century stress on community security. On the other hand, this was the point of contact between the two working principles—release of energy and control of circumstance—which dominated the character of nineteenth-century law.

We can chart shifts in time among principal and secondary preoccupations of public policy involving resort to law to shape environment. Several successions and overlaps of emphasis appear.

Years	Principal & (Secondary) Concepts of Challenge of Environment	Principal & (Secondary) Areas of Legal Response
1620–1750	Physical–Social	Community strength and security
1750–1776	Social	Political organization to release colonial energies
1776–1800	Social	Constitution making: political organization to release private individual and group energies
1800–1870	Physical–Social	Communications, credit, and national markets, as frame for release of private individual and group energies
(1820–1877)	(Social)	(Sectional balance in federalism)
(1840–1900)	(Social–Personal)	(Humanitarianism and conservation of human resources)
1870–1900	Social	Balance of power: for wider sharing of freedom of choice Community strength and security, by rationalization of social processes

Functionally, in relation to the evolution of policy, the constitution making years, 1776–1800, belong with the nineteenth century. The challenge of social environment, in terms of the organization of political power, then captured our imagination and best talent. Clashes of economic interest influenced constitution making. But at this point the focus was not so much on economics as on the politics of the economy. The contrast was sharp with the temper of 1820–1870, when the focus was on trading, speculation, and capital accumulation, and politics was on the whole impatiently dealt with. There are symbols of the times in the different careers of men who had as much in common in talent and ambition as Hamilton, Webster, and Carnegie. Hamilton found natural expression almost wholly in high politics; the disappointing ambiguity of Webster's career traced to his inability to define his role in mid-century, as man of politics or man of business; Carnegie had the better fortune to be of a generation when the issue was for the time resolved—the market was then the obvious magnet for top talent as clearly as was the forum in Hamilton's years.

The generation of constitution making was concerned to arm government with positive power; the sweeping character of legislative authority under the first state constitutions marked this. At this point release-of-energy policy found expression, significantly, in statutes as much as in constitutional provisions, for example, in legislation abolishing feudal land tenure. Though the Federal Constitution showed the full tide of the counter-movement to limit the legislative branch, it created a government empowered to play a strong, affirmative role in events. This central government had broadly defined authority to tax and to spend as means to affect the flow of resources. In its authority over foreign relations and commerce among the several states, over the money supply, and over bankruptcy it had means to give form to the market. It controlled the property of the United States; this power involved peculiar potentialities for direction of national growth because of the critically important agreement by which the states released to the nation their western land claims. Finally, the authority of the general government to admit new states to the Union enabled it to establish a political framework large enough for the fullest realization of our economic and social possibilities.

Despite this array of power, the national government played a relatively limited part in shaping our life during the first half of the century. Its most important role concerned the workings of federalism, as it confronted the problems of the balance of nation, states, and sections. Though economic and social interests were in the background, the problems of federalism were primarily political—problems of the organization of power. Federalism is the one area of early nineteenth-century concerns in which one can confidently say the focus was on political objectives. The fact testifies to the unique quality of the problems of federalism, which made it impossible to ignore them or to treat them routinely.

The creation and preservation of the Union were the first and most potent of our nineteenth-century uses of law to shape the social environment. National security and strength were important reasons for Union. But in two outstanding aspects Union also expressed the policy of controlling environment to increase private liberties. First, Madison urged, among the numerous advantages promised by a well-constructed Union, none deserves to be more accurately developed than its tendency to break and control the violence of faction. . . . [T]he same advantage which a republic has over a democracy, in controlling the effects of factions, is enjoyed by a large over a small republic—is enjoyed by the Union over the states composing it. Does the advantage consist in the substitution of representatives whose enlightened views and virtuous sentiments render them superior to local prejudices and to schemes of injustice? It will not be denied that the representation of the Union will be most likely to possess these requisite endowments. Does it consist in the greater security afforded by a greater variety of parties, against the event of any one party being able to outnumber and oppress the rest? In an equal degree does the increased variety of parties comprised within the Union, increase this security. Does it, in fine, consist in the greater obstacles opposed to the concert and accomplishment of the secret wishes of an unjust and interested majority? Here, again, the extent of the Union gives it the most palpable advantage.[9]

The creation of a balance of power, then, is a fundamental way in which we may use law to fashion the social framework. Specifically, we sought through Union to establish a broad base and diverse sources of national authority. Thus we would enlarge private liberty by reducing the likelihood that any narrow interest could capture government to the oppression of others. The principle broke down tragically in 1861 before pressures of feeling and a drift of policy which still elude full understanding. But even the principal philosopher of sectional autonomy saw the problem as one of shaping a balance of social forces through the legal organization of power. "Power can only be resisted by power— and tendency by tendency," said Calhoun. Extension of the suffrage was the first principle we had employed to achieve such a domestic balance of power as would enlarge liberty: "[T]he responsibility of the rulers to the ruled, through the right of suffrage, is the indispensable and primary principle in the *foundation* of a constitutional government." But this was not enough. Diverse special interests would strive by adroit alliance to bring about a majority vote, to the oppression of others, unless further legal arrangements preserved the balance of power. There was but one way in which the balance could finally be kept. This was

by taking the sense of each interest or portion of the community, which may be unequally and injuriously affected by the action of the government, separately, through its own majority, or in some other way by which its voice may be fairly expressed; and to require the consent of each interest, either to put or to keep the government in action.[10]

Calhoun's formula, of a sectional veto on national policy through representation in a multi-headed executive, would surely have proved impracticable. The war relegated his contrivance to the political museums. But it did not settle the question whether there might be some form of sectional veto. Nor did it destroy the relevance of Calhoun's analysis of the problems posed by diversity of interests, which took on new point with the emergence of a different type of organized pressure group toward the end of the century. We shall return to this. Here it suffices to note that a classic emphasis in early nineteenth-century public policy thus approved affirmative use of law to mould the social environment into a decent, viable balance of power for the greater liberty of private individuals and groups.[11]

In the years 1800–1877 the problem of sectional balance within the federal system stands out as the one area of prime political emphasis. Otherwise our preoccupation ceased to be with political organization. With relative impatience and superficiality we thence attended to the making of constitutions for new states. Generally, we felt, we had finished fashioning our principles of power organization by about 1800; now we could attend to the more urgent and interesting business of opening up the continent.

Court decisions showed one aspect of this focus on the economy as they built a body of doctrine which expressed faith in release of energy. If we turn to the session laws of the states, and in less measure to the United States Statutes at Large, we find practical evidence of our second working principle. It was natural that legislators rather than judges should be the prime exponents of the policy of shaping environment to enlarge men's range of choice. This called for more general and novel policy making than common law tradition envisaged as within the scope of judicial power. The scale of situations, as well as their novelty, invited an agency which could respond more readily and with a greater range of invention to community pressures than could courts within the confines of lawsuits. Measures to shape environment almost always involved direct or indirect compulsion over allocation of community resources; the legislature's control of the purse meant that it would play the central role in developing this use of law

From the years of the Cumberland Road and the Erie Canal (1806, 1817) to those of the Granger revolt in the seventies, nineteenth-century state legislation showed preoccupation with communications, credit, and the promotion of an increased scale for economic activity. These statute books present an unfamiliar pattern of emphasis to anyone who in conventional common-law fashion equates "law" with what is in the Reports. Contract was the main field of judges' creative activity in these years; within that frame of reference, release of private energy was the dominant working policy. But contemporary legislation centered on other subjects than the familiar contract, property, and tort law. What was behind this legislative preoccupation with transport and intelligence (canals, turnpikes, railroads, river improvements, telegraph, and telephone), finance (banks, currency, interest rates, and insurance), and the legal guarantee of broad areas for economic maneuver?

With our basic problems of constitution making apparently behind us, our imagination and energy had been captured by the renewed challenge of the open continent. The most obvious challenge was that of physical environment—posed by the facts of distance and scarcity of means relative to opportunities. But the problem was equally one of social situation. The physical facts carried a peculiarly intense challenge to us because the times had committed us to the market and the division of labor as prime principles of social organization. The imperative logic of the market and the division of labor called for operations over such enlarged areas of dealing, on such a scale of investment, as to raise the facts of distance and scarcity to first concern.

Resort to law to enlarge and protect the areas of free movement of trade and finance presented problems of federalism. We relied on federal organization to create a broad-based domestic balance of power. That was an emphasis natural to the political focus of the generation of constitution making. It was significant of changed directions in mid–nineteenth-century public policy that Marshall's commerce clause opinions of the 1820's had meaning largely in terms of economic goals. Within the federal framework, we would create and protect nationwide or multistate free trade areas to form an environment spacious enough for the most ambitious growth which private individuals or groups could contrive.

This area of law provided the outstanding exception to the predominance of legislation in our control-of-environment policy. It was the Court, and especially Marshall, more than the framers or pamphleteers of the Constitution, and more than the Congress, who gave durable content to this aspect of federal policy. This remained so, though the Marshall opinions blueprinted an active role for Congress in defining and protecting national free trade. Congress might license the conduct of interstate commerce, and the Court would treat its licenses as passports, overriding any tariff or monopoly with which a state sought to protect local interest. In *Gibbons* v. *Ogden*, Marshall found such a grant of free passage implied in a coastal shipping license issued under authority of an act of Congress; in *Brown* v. *Maryland,* he found a license to import implied in the exaction of a federal tariff.[12] In both instances, it seems plain, Marshall adopted a strained interpretation of the meaning of the federal statutes. The degree of his contrivance underlined his deliberate effort to fashion an apparatus of legal controls.

This became still more obvious when his dicta opened another avenue of federal restraint on parochialism. The mere grant of the commerce power to Congress, Marshall indicated, involved some displacement of state power. Here, apparently, the Court would be the active agent of federal policy; in this role, it would set aside state legislation which in its judgment might unduly confine the play of economic energy. Federal protection would embrace all the conditions important to the existence of broad markets:

The genius and character of the whole government seem to be, that its action is to be applied to all the external concerns of the nation, and to those internal concerns which affect the States generally; but not to those which are completely within a particular State, which do not affect other States, and with which it is not necessary to interfere, for the purpose of executing some of the general powers of the government.[13]

Within its realm, federal authority meant full and affirmative power to act for the positive accomplishment of national policy, unhampered by the Tenth Amendment or any limit implied in the mere coexistence of the states:

If, as has always been understood, the sovereignty of congress, though limited to specified objects, is plenary as to those objects, the power over commerce with foreign nations, and among the several States, is vested in congress as absolutely as it would be in a single government, having in its constitution the same restrictions on the exercise of the power as are found in the constitution of the United States.[14]

However, it was not until the second half of the century that we really put federalism to work for the uses which Marshall had outlined. Inventions in techniques of production, management, and finance then enabled business to occupy markets and build capital structures of unprecedented scale. The new business dynamics found a hospitable environment in the broad field of maneuver which the law of the federal system guaranteed.

It was the Court which continued to play the lead in shaping the freedom of multi-state areas for economic movement. The threat of interstate tariff wars took on new proportions when local interest learned more sophisticated methods of burdening foreign competition, and fresh dangers appeared as states became aware that the richer flow of commerce in widened markets offered promising new sources of revenue. The decisive period was in the seventies and eighties, when the Court consolidated the policy and role which Marshall had outlined; the pace of doctrinal development in these years measured the rapidity of growth of multi-state marketing.

There were two lines of development. The narrower one involved assertion of judicial authority to upset state taxes or regulations which discriminated against interstate commerce. *Welton* v. *Missouri* (1875) at last firmly established this police function of the Court. Mr. Justice Field's opinion declared the positive responsibility, as well as authority, of the central government to fashion the legal conditions of a free national market:

The power to regulate conferred by [the commerce] . . . clause upon Congress is one without limitation; and to regulate commerce is to prescribe rules by which it shall be governed—that is, the conditions upon which it shall be conducted; to determine how far it shall be free and untrammelled, how far it shall be burdened by duties and imposts, and how far it shall be prohibited.

. . . [T]hat portion of commerce with foreign countries and between the States which consists in the transportation and exchange of commodities is of national importance, and admits and requires uniformity of regulation. The very object of investing this power in the General Government was to insure this uniformity against discriminating State legislation. . . .

. . . [T]he commercial power continues until the commodity has ceased to be the subject of discriminating legislation by reason of its foreign character. That power protects it, even after it has entered the State, from any burdens imposed by reason of its foreign origin. . . . The fact that Congress has not seen fit to prescribe any specific rules to govern inter-State commerce does not affect the question. Its inaction on this subject, when considered with reference to its legislation with respect to foreign commerce, is equivalent to a declaration that inter-State commerce shall be free and untrammelled. . . .[15]

However, discrimination was only the more obvious threat which localism opposed to expanding economic energies. The new scale of business was both its opportunity and its point of vulnerability. It was exposed to the view and reach of numerous taxing and regulatory authorities; though their exactions were not discriminatory, their cumulative burdens or their inconsistencies might destroy practical freedom to test out multi-state areas of economic operation. Even a nondiscriminatory state tax was invalid if it was a tax upon interstate transportation. "It is of national importance," said the Court in the *Case of the State Freight Tax,* "that there should be but one regulating power" over the general subject of interstate transportation. Again, the federal balance should create a favorable environment for the release of energy:

. . . [F]or if one State can directly tax persons or property passing through it, or tax them indirectly by levying a tax upon their transportation, every other may, and thus commercial intercourse between States remote from each other may be destroyed. The produce of Western States may thus be effectually excluded from Eastern markets, for though it might bear the imposition of a single tax, it would be crushed under the load of many. It was to guard against the possibility of such commercial embarrassments, no doubt, that the power of regulating commerce among the States was conferred upon the Federal government. . . .[16]

The logic of its policy dictated that the Court should likewise intervene to limit regulatory activity of the states where regulation, though nondiscriminatory, carried the danger of cumulative or inconsistent burdens. Mr. Justice Miller's opinion in the *Wabash Railway* case (1886) reflected the sense that a new business dynamics demanded the creative protection of Union:

It cannot be too strongly insisted upon that the right of continuous transportation from one end of the country to the other is essential in modern times to that freedom of commerce from the restraints which the State might choose to impose upon it, that the commerce clause was intended to secure. . . . [I]t would be a very feeble and almost useless provision, but poorly adapted to secure the entire freedom of commerce among the States which was deemed essential to a more perfect union by the framers of the Constitution, if, at every stage of the transportation of goods and chattels through the country, the State within whose limits a part of this transportation must be done could impose regulations concerning the price, compensation, or taxation, or any other restrictive regulation interfering with and seriously embarrassing this commerce.[17]

Railroad and other transport cases bulk large in the creation of late– nineteenth-century commerce clause law. But the opinions indicate that the prime object of protection was the general flow of interstate trade which the railroads facilitated. The Court saw itself as shaping the general environment of multi-state business. This may help explain the curious divergence between the vigor with which the Justices guaranteed free multi-state areas of maneuver where state taxation or regulation fell on interstate transactions, whether of individuals or of corporations, and the contemporary hardening of the doctrine that a state might bar or set arbitrary conditions to the entry of a foreign corporation seeking to do business within the state. The idea of the corporation as an instrument of privilege or monopoly thus made itself felt in policy long past the time when the corporation had become a common, necessary means to occupy the broad areas of economic maneuver which commerce clause law had opened up. The rigor of the exclusionary power so conceded to the states was the more striking because so far as the Court felt able to use its own discretion it early accepted the corporation as a normal instrument of the new scale of business. It developed the odd fictions which allowed corporate litigants access to federal courts under the diversity of citizenship jurisdiction. It presumed that, by comity, a state allowed a corporation to do business within it unless state law clearly declared to the contrary. Not until the twentieth century, however, did the Court develop the doctrine of "unconstitutional conditions" to add to the protections of multi-state economic areas the reasonable assurance of a right to use the corporate form of business.[18]

The Justices reflected some uneasiness about the scope of their policy making under the commerce clause by their reiterated appeals to the authority of the framers and the implied commands of the Congress. The general silence of Congress over the years from 1872 on may at least imply Congressional content that the Justices handle these difficult issues, however dubious the evidence that Congress ratified any particulars of the body of judge-made law.

It is clear enough that Congress made little explicit use of the licensing power as Marshall had outlined its potentialities. The Act of August 31, 1852, licensed bridges across the Ohio River at Wheeling. The Supreme Court recognized this as binding, though before this enactment the Court had ordered the bridges abated as public nuisances which contravened Congressional regulations of navigation and hence could not be authorized by the Virginia statute approving their construction.[19] The act of June 15, 1866, cautiously exercised the protective licensing function; enacted to override New Jersey's grant to the Camden & Amboy Railroad of a monopoly between New York and Philadelphia, this statute declared that connecting carriers had the right to transport passengers and goods from state to state.[20] Of course, Congress also gave federal charters to several transcontinental railroads. Sustaining the constitutionality of these acts, the Court spoke in terms suggestive of the protective licensing power and again emphasizing the challenge which a changing economy posed, to provide an adequate legal framework for growth:

The power to construct, or to authorize individuals or corporations to construct, national highways and bridges from State to State, is essential to the complete control and regulation of interstate commerce. Without authority in Congress to establish and maintain such highways and bridges, it would be without authority to regulate one of the most important adjuncts of commerce. This power in former times was exerted to a very limited extent, the Cumberland or National Road being the most notable instance. Its exertion was but little called for, as commerce was then mostly conducted by water, and many of our statesmen entertained doubts as to the existence of the power to establish ways of communication by land. But since, in consequence of the expansion of the country, the multiplication of its products, and the invention of railroads and locomotion by steam, land transportation has so vastly increased, a sounder consideration of the subject has prevailed, and led to the conclusion that Congress has plenary power over the whole subject.[21]

Though the Court treated a federal railroad charter as a federal franchise which a state might not tax, it does not appear that Congress had particularly regarded the charters as protective licenses; these federal corporations were useful instruments to express Congressional resolution of sectional rivalry and to receive grants of public lands in aid of railroad construction. Where construction did not run through federal territories, Congress conditioned the railroads' entry into states on the grant of state permission or relied on state co-operation through grant of local charters for particular divisions of the roads.[22]

In 1877 the Court held that a federal statute of July 24, 1866, protected the extension of an interstate telegraph line into Florida, overriding a state-granted monopoly to a local company. "It cannot for a moment be doubted," said Mr. Chief Justice Waite, "that this powerful agency of commerce and inter-communication comes within the controlling power of Congress, certainly as against hostile State legislation." The government of the United States has a "peculiar duty . . . to protect one part of the country from encroachments by another upon the national rights which belong to all." [23] Again, however, it was the Court more than Congress which treated the federal statute as a protective license against state action; the Congressional discussion indicates that Congress had been mainly concerned to prevent private monopoly in the interstate telegraph business.[24] The Interstate Commerce Act of 1887 marked the entry of Congress into the full-fledged use of its positive authority. At a later point an important justification of federal regulation was that it would prevent local interest from loading its costs onto interstate transport.[25] But it was the complete regulatory gap left when the *Wabash*

Railway decision barred state control of interstate rail rates and practices which originally impelled Congress to pass the act of 1887; in its inception that statute was not primarily an exercise of the protective license function.[26]

There were institutional reasons why the Court, rather than Congress, led in protecting multi-state areas of economic maneuver. It was a bold step when the Court originally seized the initiative to define public policy of such scope. But once it had done this, the Court was better adapted than the Congress for the detailed protection of private freedom. Tenure and professional tradition insulated the Justices from local or special pressures to which Congressmen were more vulnerable. A lawsuit required definition of issues in their most concrete context, and this gave assurance that policy would stay close to reality. The availability of a judicial remedy was important to overcoming the institutional inertia that always handicaps vindication of individual freedoms. The Court sat more often than Congress, and one who could finance a lawsuit and find competent counsel was armed for a fair fight there, whereas he might have to organize a lobby to press through a bill. However, these were all advantages primarily in the elaboration and application of policy. By mid–twentieth century there was new, heightened competition among governments for revenue and between industries for markets. These circumstances finally created sufficient dissatisfaction over the working relations of law and the national free trade ideal to bring increasing demands that Congress intervene to re-examine and redefine general policy.

Federal law might shape an environment favorable to the existence of multi-state areas of free economic movement. But the record of policy was not without ambiguity. One may speculate a bit when Mr. Justice Field speaks so ardently for the positive responsibility of federal law, where the immediate effect is to remove a state regulation of business without putting a federal regulation in its place. There may be similar overtones here to those one heard earlier, when Story saw a broad reach of exclusive federal power over commerce at a time when this would probably mean in practice neither federal nor state control.[27] The *Child Labor* cases at a later day taught lawyers that the commerce clause might be put to the same substantial uses as due process doctrine, to relieve business of regulation.[28]

But if laissez faire infused some later commerce clause law, this does not seem a concealed motive in the nineteenth-century development we have been considering. There was a mass of contemporary state commercial regulation which was throughout accepted as normal and lawful.[29] With consistent caution the Court refused to adopt extreme doctrine as to the "exclusive" range of national commerce power, in years when it was politically most unlikely that Congress would fill the gap left by the end of state regulations.[30] Through the seventies and eighties, when the Justices definitively assumed the role of protecting national free trade under the commerce clause, the future of the Fourteenth Amendment as a limitation on state police power remained in doubt. "For protection against abuses by legislatures the people must resort to the polls, not to the courts," the majority had said in 1877 in *Munn* v. *Illinois*. Not before the *Railroad Commission Cases* of 1886 was it clear that the Court would act to check state regulatory power.[31] And it was well into the twentieth century before the Court began to withdraw from its firm nineteenth-century position, that a state had unchecked discretion in admitting or conditioning the admission of a foreign corporation to do business within its boundaries, notwithstanding the commerce clause or any other provision of the Federal Constitution, including the new Fourteenth Amendment.[32] Due process doctrine was scarcely so thriving in the seventies and eighties as to have surplus energy to spill over into commerce clause channels.

State legal policy presented analogies to the use of federal law to shape an environment favorable for economic growth. If multi-state areas of economic maneuver permitted a new scale of operations and productivity, so also a state-wide market was essential to growth beyond the capacities of county economies. The first, and the outstanding, development of state legal policy to this end concerned transportation. However much responsibility it delegated to local governments for public roads administration, the state legislature typically kept careful hold of authority to designate routes and impose on local governments the costs of roads which crossed county lines.[33] The legislature might delegate to local interests the discretion to build milldams on country streams. But it held jealously to the authority to license particular works on navigable waters under stipulations protecting through traffic. The guarantees of free passage were usually drawn in very general terms and lacked adequate sanctions for enforcement; undoubtedly they must be assessed as often purely formal acknowledgments of the general interest. Yet there was impressive consistency in these statutory declarations of public policy; were they only acknowledgments, yet they attested a substantial opinion that law should protect the conditions essential to maintain broad areas for economic movement within the state.[34]

The most important state legislative policy of this kind concerned railroad taxes. Taxation of railroad property by local government units would likely produce inconsistent bases of valuation and competition for revenue among the taxing counties or towns, which would seriously hamper development of facilities critically important for the general economy. Of course, railroad lobbies sought special tax status for their own gain. In the early years, when communities were more anxious to see the railroads built than to scrutinize what the railroads asked, it was the roads' initiative which won for them the right to pay the state a single, centrally assessed property tax, or a tax or license fee based on income, in lieu of all other levies. But this grew into standard policy through the later, turbulent years of railroad politics. The fact indicates that there was a solid basis in general interest for special, centralized tax treatment of these facilities; and, indeed, this became the pattern for taxation of other facilities important to the framework of the economy.[35]

As trade became more mobile and expanding business sought wider markets, local interests resorted to municipal licensing, regulation, or taxation to raise tariff walls about home-town enterprise. For the same ends, local merchant interests also pressed to enlarge the range of state legislation regulating hawkers and peddlers. State courts showed more energy than state legislatures in resisting these thrusts of localism. The judges were sometimes vague in defining the doctrine by which they upset burdens or discriminations against state-wide traders, but the equal protection clause of the Fourteenth Amendment, or its counterpart in state constitutions, ultimately proved to be their standard recourse. This area of state policy had a late nineteenth-century growth, natural in view of the limits of business in most states in the earlier years; it was to take on more importance when twentieth-century autos, trucks, and hard-surfaced roads made local enterprise much more vulnerable to broad-area competition.[36]

But it meant little that law guaranteed state-wide and multi-state fields for economic growth if we lacked means to exploit these opportunities. We felt the challenge of our physical and social environment most sharply, in the first half of the century, in a constant awareness of capital scarcity. There was no lack of the raw materials of economic growth; indeed, the abundance of land, timber, minerals, and water-power created a very different problem of public policy by dangerously retarding development of a sensible social cost accounting; waste had little meaning when resources seemed inexhaustible. The one basic capital resource we lacked was people. Otherwise, the scarcity of which we were acutely conscious, because it constantly tantalized by contrast to the promise of the continent, was scarcity of fluid, mobile capital, scarcity of present purchasing power to buy labor, equipment, and time.

Law helped shape an economic environment of broad multi-state and state-wide markets chiefly by regulating behavior—behavior of political units and of private individuals and groups. Law responded to the pervasive sense of capital scarcity chiefly by affecting the allocation of economic resources. In part it did this by underwriting the release-of-energy principle. This role of law centered on private volition: law guaranteed and protected individuals and groups in their private planning and execution, and where it brought its force to bear it was to extend the reach of private will by lending it legal power to enforce its decisions and fulfill its expectations. But in the first half of the century we also used the compulsion of law directly to affect the allocation of resources; government took the responsibility of channelling the flow of assets in some key areas of the economy and employed a variety of compulsions to this end.

The impact of nineteenth-century legal policy on direction of the flow of capital was of two very distinct types over two rather distinct periods. From about 1800 to 1870, we can see a pattern of surprisingly deliberate and self-conscious policy—deliberate enough to constitute a working principle, that law should increase men's liberty by enlarging their practical range of options in the face of limiting circumstance. From about 1870 to 1900, we can see an unpatterned, radically important drift and default of policy, through which the legal order profoundly affected the accumulation and control of capital and thus contributed to creating a new challenge of social environment to liberty. Of course, the boundaries of the two periods were not in fact sharply defined; implementation of the policies of the first period reached forward into the eighties, and the trends of the second period gathered momentum in the late fifties and through the war years.

Over the first three-quarters of the century, we used law to help determine priorities among competing uses of our scarce working capital. Four priorities decisions stand out. Listed in descending order according to breadth and firmness of foundation in public opinion, these were the decisions to promote by law the allocation of capital to transport, to the development of commercial agriculture, to the fostering of credit facilities, and to the encouragement of industry. These were decisions expressed almost wholly through legislation; so far as the courts involved themselves here in basic policy as distinct from the implementation of policy, it was to put brakes to legislative enthusiasm.

Public support might shift from turnpikes to canals and river improvements and then to railroads; and after the first generation of ebullient confidence in promoters' promises, there likely followed a generation of disillusionment and effort to withdraw from commitments. But during each upcurve of enthusiasm there could be no doubt that people wanted government to mobilize resources to build means of cheap, bulk transportation. Sectional rivalries within the nation and within individual states only emphasized the common conviction that communications were the secret of growth and opportunity and hence demanded a positive legal policy in each market area. The biographer of a Massachusetts railroad pioneer comments on the problems of launching the new enterprise in a fashion revealing of the temper of public opinion at the outset of construction:

A charter was to be obtained, and, as yet, no charter for a railroad had been granted in New England. The terms of the charter, and its conditions, were to be carefully considered. The experiment was deemed to be so desirable, and at the same time, so hazardous, that the legislature were prepared to grant almost any terms that should be asked for. Mr. Jackson, on the other hand, whose faith in the success of the new mode of locomotion never faltered, was not disposed to ask for any privileges that would not be deemed moderate after the fullest success had been obtained; at the same time, the recent example of the Charles River Bridge showed the necessity of guarding, by careful provisions, the chartered rights of the stockholders.[37]

About twenty years later, in the first flush of Wisconsin enthusiasm for railroad construction, Governor Barstow urged the 1854 legislature that it had "a duty. . . . to foster. . . . and to be wary of throwing impediments in the way" of railroad construction.[38] Of course, the railroad lobbyists were busy and effective. But in the early years they had leverage because they struck a broad response in public attitudes. A Whig promoter of the Erie Railroad, Samuel B. Ruggles, in the 1830's criticized the view that government's role was merely the negative one of protecting individual life, liberty, and property. Dorfman tells that

before the road was completed, and it took practically twenty years, the company more than once was willing to sell out to the state, and Ruggles even reached a point where he argued that a large-scale enterprise like a railroad could not and should not be left to private enterprise because of insufficient capital and the dangers of stock jobbing.

The railroad was seen as one of the framework institutions of a broad liberty to be enjoyed by all:

Few in the business questioned Ruggles's statement that the construction of railroads throughout the country was the one vast democratic machine for equalizing the condition of the people. There is no truer, more honest, unterrified democrat "than the railroad, for the moment steam entered, aristocracy was doomed and the final enfranchisement of society from artificial distinctions, absolutely and effectively secured." [39]

Quick survey and sale of the public lands at low prices, or the free grant of public lands to actual settlers, were policies which held an unquestioned place in broad public opinion, second only to promotion of communications. There were sectional cleavages on the basic policy here: northeastern employers were not enthusiastic about a land policy which might draw off labor; southern political opinion was wary of western growth. However, the existence of these dissents served mainly to bear witness to the strength and wide appeal of the policy which prevailed. The original idea of a liberal public lands policy was largely political: Jefferson would foster an independent, small farmer class to guarantee the morals of politics; Jacksonian doctrine preached easy land terms to achieve social equality. But in the Mississippi Valley, where centered the driving force of the policy for quick and easy settlement, there was typically emphasis on fostering production and enlarging the practical freedom of average people by promoting an economy of family farms producing for the market.

"Agriculture . . . is our great and leading interest," Governor Farwell admonished the Wisconsin legislature of 1852,

and any measure or policy, having a tendency to embarrass or restrict the cultivation of the soil already appropriated to the purposes of husbandry, or the improvement of the lands yet vacant and unsold lying within our boundaries, I regard as militating against our best interests as a state; and on the other hand, any thing conducive to promote and encourage this branch of productive industry, and to extend its limits, is the true policy of the state. . . .

Into his analysis Farwell wove the theme of expansion of men's liberties within the hospitable environment of the United States: the letters home of friends and acquaintances already here, the political unsettlement of Europe, and the dissemination among European peoples of the knowledge of the free principles of this country could be counted on to produce a swelling immigration.

. . . [W]e are . . . called upon by every consideration of state policy, as well as patriotism and humanity—not only to have our vacant lands ready to receive them, but to extend towards them a special encouragement and protection, until they shall have made for themselves homes in the state.

However, as a practical matter land policy was basic to realizing this dream of growth and human betterment. Farwell came back to hard-headed emphasis on marketing terms:

I would much prefer that the General Government would reduce the price of our vacant lands to simply cover the cost of their survey and sale, and bring them at once into market, as an inducement to emigration from the more densely populated parts of our own country, and from foreign countries; and in this way, add to the population, wealth, and productive labor of the state; and sub-due and cultivate this rich domain, than that they should be granted to com-panies in large parcels, to build up sectional interests and subserve private purposes.[40]

As with communications development, a first generation of enthusiasm for an inadequately planned policy of quick settlement was likely to be followed by disillusionment with costs and results. This fact does not dim the impressive vigor of the original decision that we use the law's resources to shape the growth of a particular kind of agriculture in which family farms would produce for the market.[41]

During many of the years from 1800 to 1860 Bank or No Bank was the fighting issue which most colored national and state politics, apart from the sectional conflict. The issue was typically as confused as it was hot. It stirred deep emotion and sharp awareness of interest differences. Whether they were eastern merchants or financiers, or western land speculators or farmers, men saw that credit and money arrangements fundamentally affected the scope of their practical opportunities. This touched the most sensitive nerves of ambition and hope in a mobile, striving society.

In their different fashions both Whig and Jackson Democrat believed that the law must take positive responsibility for banking because this affected the framework necessary for free economic maneuver. When he played his more sober role as responsible central banker, Nicholas Biddle felt the obligation of the Second Bank of the United States to maintain the integrity of the market as an institution. Partly the Bank's task was to see to the "preservation" of the currency by "control and restriction" of the "extravagant issues of local banks." As a discount house, it should guard against "over-banking which occasions an over-trading"; to check the improvident optimism of the state banks, it should place itself "in an attitude of security and strength, so as to interpose whenever it may be necessary to protect the community." [42] On the other hand, it was the potential or realized power of the Bank thus to affect the general conditions of economic movement which stirred the fear and dislike of the Opposition. To open his attack on renewing the charter of the Second Bank of the United States, Senator Thomas Hart Benton. properly pointed out that credit and currency arrangements involved decisions affecting men's freedom. However one assesses the merits of the Senator's judgment on the Bank, there can be no doubt that he expressed a widely shared distrust and fear of this power:

I look upon the bank as an institution too great and powerful to be tolerated in a Government of free and equal laws. Its power is that of a purse; a power more potent than that of the sword; and this power it possesses to a degree and extent that will enable this bank to draw to itself too much of the political power of this Union; and too much of the individual property of the citizens of these States. . . . This mass of power, thus concentrated, thus ramified, and thus directed, must necessarily become, under a prolonged existence, the absolute monopolist of American money, the sole manufacturer of paper currency, and the sole authority (for authority it will be) to which the Federal Government, the State Governments, the great cities, corporate bodies, merchants, traders, and every private citizen, must, of necessity apply, for every loan which their exigencies may demand. "The rich ruleth the poor, and the borrower is the servant of the lender." . . .[43]

The early nineteenth-century controversy over chartering banks and defining their function, like the contemporary issue over incorporation of other business enterprises, shows the practical costs of operating without good theory. To provide a reliable medium of exchange and facilities to mobilize scarce and scattered capital for long-term investment and for short-term needs of trade and seasonal agriculture was essential to a division-of-labor, market economy. But all kinds of misconceptions confused the view of these simple requirements. Goods-minded people saw all banking as a swindle because it made money out of selling time. Men found it hard to see that a proper paper medium could better do the job of hard cash; yet on the other hand, they could not see that paper did not make wealth and that the reality back of a bill of exchange was the movement of commodities which it represented. Likewise they failed to see that the functions of note issue and discounting could be separate.

We could not get along without banks or some institutional machinery to provide a currency, and we did not. As with corporate charters, legislatures which resounded with charges against banks nonetheless wound up by creating them and authorizing their note issues. In substantial measure the law provided credit and currency facilities under its release-of-energy principle; the notoriety of the "wildcat" state banks of the second quarter of the century reminds us how far many states finally went in liberally chartering banks under no effective supervision. But we also employed the positive force of law to help mobilize and create means of credit and exchange. Some states saw opportunities to profit and to reconcile public welfare and private interest by setting up state banks as monopolies, or creating banks in which the state became a substantial investor, or exacting considerable bonus payments or obligations to lend to the state as a condition of monopolistic charters. The United States was a substantial, if minority, investor in both of the Banks of the United States, and both institutions were designed to play the semi-official role of central banks in discipline of state institutions. When the sovereign declared notes of its chartered banks to be legal tender generally, or at least for obligations owed itself, it further employed its positive power to create a financial machinery for the community.

Eventually we did learn one basic lesson: We could not deal by mere fiat with conditions that affected the whole framework and processes of shaping the social environment. Jackson tried to settle the central bank problem by a simple No. But the facts would not permit an answer by simple prohibition. The only result of the attempt was a wasteful and damaging generation of unstable credit and money. We returned to an affirmative policy when the National Banking Acts of 1863 and 1864 created something like a central banking system. In 1865 we underlined our commitment to the positive use of law to shape the financial environment when we outlawed state bank notes by putting them under a prohibitive federal tax.

Wisconsin's experience was a typical demonstration within a smaller theater, that our ultimate policy was to use the law to provide facilities of exchange. The Wisconsin constitutional convention of 1846 presented to the people a draft constitution which wholly prohibited the business of banking and banned circulation of paper money of less than twenty-dollar denomination. A broad, if rather inarticulate, opinion against the wisdom of this measure contributed to rejection of the 1846 document at the polls. Subsequently the Wisconsin voters accepted the handiwork of the 1848 constitutional convention, including authority given the legislature after approval at a public referendum to enact special or general banking laws which must be ratified by further referendum. In the outcome the deliberately cumbersome procedure served only to emphasize how far the anti-bank zealots misjudged the deeper demands of public opinion; the people promptly approved legislative action and then ratified a general banking law providing state supervision. This act governed Wisconsin banking until the end of the century; in 1902 a constitutional amendment empowered the legislature to pass general banking laws without separate submission to the people.[44]

The protective tariff for industry represented another nineteenth-century use of law to affect allocation of resources. Of the instances so far discussed, this was the last to become well fixed in policy. Through 1850 emphasis wavered between revenue and protection; not until 1861–1864, with the South absent from Congress and the Republican Party firmly committed, did protection become the firm-set objective. Among the public policies we have discussed, protection had the least solid support in broad opinion; it was more clearly identified with specialized interests than with provision of a framework for the general economy. The pattern of interests crisscrossed and shifted in time: the South could always be considered in opposition; the West could sometimes be attracted to high tariffs linked to internal improvements finance, but this did not prove a lasting attraction; in the North the issue of protection was fought between industrialists and merchants. Moreover, despite the fervor with which particular industries sought protection, the record is by no means clear how far the tariff in fact contributed to the growth of protected industries.

With all these qualifications, the case of the protective tariff still belongs in our catalog, if only because its proponents attested the general readiness to use law to shape environment for greater freedom by invoking this belief in their behalf. "When all the different kinds of industry obtain in a community, each individual can find his proper element and can call into activity the whole vigor of his nature," argued Hamilton;

. . . and the community is benefited by the services of its respective members, in the manner in which each can serve it with most effect. If there be anything in a remark often to be met with, namely, that there is, in the genius of the people of this country, a peculiar aptitude for mechanic improvements, it would operate as a forcible reason for giving opportunities to the exercise of that species of talent, by the propagation of manufacturers.

To cherish and stimulate the activity of the human mind, by multiplying the objects of enterprise, is not among the least considerable of the expedients by which the wealth of a nation may be promoted. . . . Every new scene which is opened to the busy nature of man to rouse and exert itself is the addition of a new energy to the general stock of effort. The spirit of enterprise, useful and prolific as it is, must necessarily be contracted or expanded, in proportion to the simplicity or variety of the occupations and productions which are to be found in a society. It must be less in a nation of mere cultivators than in a nation of cultivators and merchants; less in a nation of cultivators and merchants than in a nation of cultivators, artificers, and merchants.[45]

Implicit in these various legal policies affecting resources allocation was a working principle of directing capital to points where the greatest multiplier effects might be anticipated. To this end we also used law directly or indirectly to enforce the mobilization of capital.

To increase the net capital at our command, we encouraged capital imports. The most important import of foreign capital was in people. Immigrants brought cash and goods with them, but probably on balance this was offset by expenses of our tourists abroad. The invaluable net addition to capital was in the hands, energies, and brains of the immigrants. When hard times made competition felt in the labor market there were waves of sentiment to limit immigration, but the clear-cut general policy of the nineteenth century was to encourage it. As a federal policy, we left an open door and used the authority of federal power to limit states or local governments in their regulation of entry. The states often extended the vote to the foreign born in anticipation of their obtaining citizenship. Both nation and states sold public lands cheaply to induce immigration, and this was also one object of public subsidy of canal and railroad construction. States set up immigration commissions to publicize abroad the advantages they offered for settlement and sent agents to key ports to assist immigrants with information and to guard them against fraud. The deep-moving currents which brought unprecedented immigration to the United States in the nineteenth century originated in political and economic circumstances across the water; our open-door policy simply accepted these opportunities for increase in our population, and our promotional efforts only seconded the pressure of outside events. Nevertheless, our reaction in policy to this movement of people indicated our operative notions of the proper role of law. On this point the record was clear: Legal policy should affirmatively encourage the increase of our human capital.[46]

We took affirmative steps also to encourage foreign investment in the United States. This had been an objective of the assumption of the Revolutionary debts. It was a reason for strengthening the fiscal powers of the central government under the new Federal Constitution and erecting barriers to state debt repudiation by giving jurisdiction to federal courts in all cases arising under treaties and in cases in which a foreigner was a party. Foreign investment was originally welcomed in the First and Second Banks of the United States, though its presence became a count in later indictments of those institutions. Starting with the Erie Canal, state internal improvement projects underwritten by the tax power provided tangible foci for foreign funds. In the depression of 1837 state defaults damaged our credit abroad. But in a later generation the Supreme Court exerted itself to a questionable degree to devise means of using the federal courts to enforce bondholders' claims against local governments which had lent their credit in aid of railroad building.[47]

Government had two principal means to affect the directions of domestic investment—its own property (the public lands) and its powers to tax and to spend. Waste, fraud, and incompetence on a large scale marked the administration of national and state public land policies. But there was little faltering in definition of central policy. This great public lands resource should be used to direct the course of economic growth by grants to aid transportation improvements and by marketing policies to promote immigration and settlement to build a family-farm agriculture. The public lands might have been marketed primarily to meet the ordinary revenue needs of government. This was the policy at the outset of our national life, but it was abandoned by the 1830's in the face of settlers' pressure and the broad opinion favoring promotional use of the lands. The change emphasizes that a deliberate choice was made here in using law to shape the social environment.[48]

The power to tax is inherently a power to direct allocation of a part of community economic resources. This is so even when the objects of public expenditure are narrow and conventional. But nineteenth-century policy did not confine the spending of public revenue to maintaining minimum police functions. The national government used its revenues from taxes as well as from public lands to build lighthouses and improve harbors, particularly at first in aid of coastal navigation. It was the consciousness that government was thus reallocating assets to promote commerce that provoked the pointed demands of the West for its share. The attitude for which Henry Clay spoke in his "American System" was that reflected in the tart tones of Wisconsin's Governor Barstow when in 1855 he urged that the legislature memorialize Congress for more liberal rivers and harbors aids:

Thus far we have had but little to thank the general government for, save those benefits resulting from democratic institutions, and of which we are all the common recipients, saving those embraced in donations for special purposes. We have paid into the United States treasury the fixed value of every acre of land now or heretofore owned by the state or its citizens, and of this amount thus promptly advanced, the country has received the benefit. . . .[49]

Of course, this viewpoint easily degenerated into "pork barrel" politics; but the stubborn tenacity of pork barrel practice attests that we accepted in our working philosophy the role of public expenditure in directing the flow of assets.

The states made some direct grants or investments of public funds in canal and railroad companies. But their large-scale use of the tax power was indirect—by allowing tax exemptions or creating a tax structure tailored to the convenience of a particular industry or employing tax revenues to back public credit to mobilize funds for internal improvements investments. The strict public debt limitations which became standard in state constitutions after mid-century bear witness to the excesses of this policy and its partial repudiation.

However, the mingled pressure of promoters' lobbies and public ambitions was great enough to find another outlet. From the fifties until the eighties, the tax-supported credit of municipalities backed further railroad development and to some extent subsidized the growth of local industry. That the positive compulsion of law was here allocating resources was made dramatically clear when bilked or disappointed municipalities later sought to avoid payment of their railroad aid obligations. In one of the most strong-handed chapters of judicial policy making, the United States Supreme Court put the whole force of the federal courts behind enforcement of these public debts, holding municipalities to the strictest reading of their liability and sanctioning federal writs to compel them to levy taxes to pay interest and principal.

Constitutional and statutory restrictions finally curbed municipal venturing. But the most striking limits were set by the state courts, as they developed the doctrine that tax funds might constitutionally be used only for what the judges would define as "public purposes." This doctrine was not usually invoked to bar aid to railroad construction, but it did operate in the latter years of the century substantially to bar public aid grants or loans of public credit to subsidize industry. However, the familiar pendulum movement of policy is apparent in definitions of proper uses of the public purse to promote economic growth. The twentieth century would conclude that public finance had been unwisely straitjacketed in the reaction to nineteenth-century excesses; formal constitutional change was slight, but twentieth-century legislative and judicial practice and doctrine tended to relax the "public purpose" limitation and to apply a strong presumption of constitutionality in favor of using public finance to underwrite the stability and expansion of the economy. The depression of the 1930's enormously strengthened, but did not initiate this swing back toward promotional use of public finance.[50]

More striking and novel than government's direct use of its fiscal powers in the first seventy-five years of the century was the extent to which it lent its compulsion to enforce allocations made by certain private individuals and groups. In practical effect, the law delegated a taxing power to private decision makers to help them mobilize capital for communications and credit development.

A novel development of nineteenth-century public policy was the delegation of the power of eminent domain to private corporations, generally in the field of communications or water power development. The power was particularly essential to completing the purchase of a right of way without hindrance or blackmail by individual property owners. Resort to eminent domain might stretch promoters' capital by saving them from paying high prices for land. Conversely, whatever the courts' vague formulae meant in practice, they meant at least that the law deprived the property owner of his ordinary right to set his own price; neither the distinctive value of the property to the owner nor that to the taker should measure compensation, but some figure ultimately set by a legal agency under a flexible, more or less objective measure of "fair market value." The unfailing care with which promoters included the eminent domain privilege in any charter which could be deemed of sufficient public interest to warrant it attests the estimation in which the power was held. Typical impatience with property owners' hindrance of facilities important for the general economy was expressed by the majority of the Wisconsin court which in 1849 sustained a delegation of eminent domain authority to developers of water power:

No tyranny has been found more odious in the older states than is sometimes exhibited in the pertinacious obstinacy of one man, who pursues his common-law right of resisting the occupation of his land, perhaps of some small and insignificant but indispensable portion, for the purpose of a mill. The graceless privilege of commencing daily suits for the daily infringement of constitutional rights is often less detrimental to the enterprising individual, who may be its victim, than to the community, who are common sufferers. The statute which cuts off the common-law privilege of such a man to indulge in litigious malice, and which secures to him ample compensation by a single action for his property taken for public use, is surely benign in its effects, and harmonious with the spirit if not the letter of the constitution. Such a law, also, by inviting capital into the interior of the state, by encouraging enterprise and diffusing the conveniences of social life, enhances the value of land, advances its settlement, and promotes general civilization.[51]

A strong dissent objected to the extent of the public power thus delegated to private decision makers. But in 1854 the trend of policy was so firmly set that the Wisconsin court could say:

The time has gone by, when it is proper to discuss or question, judicially, the power of the legislature to exercise the right of eminent domain resting in the sovereignty of the state, by delegation to incorporated companies. However powerful may heretofore have been the adverse array of logical argument, the suggestions of cautious expediency, or the jealousy of personal rights, it has long since yielded to the irresistible tide of progressive improvement, and been lost in the wake of judicial authority.[52]

Somewhat analogous to the effect of the delegated eminent domain power was the result of the bargaining leeway which railroad promoters usually enjoyed in laying out routes. The absence of any firm state planning enhanced the roads' practical power to exact capital contributions from localities as the price of a favorable lay-out of the right of way. To some extent, however, this railroad bargaining strength was offset where the state held aid lands as its bargaining counter. And the courts might at least hold the roads to their agreements by relieving local governments of their aid promises where the railroad violated its undertakings as to route.[53]

Another important way in which the law in effect delegated to private hands powers to compel mobilization of capital was by granting the right to fix tolls to recipients of franchises for turnpikes and plankroads, canals, river improvements, railroads, and water power developments. The services rendered were usually practical necessities to the customers; the charges were thus inherently somewhat of a compulsory exaction, as the legislatures acknowledged when they stipulated for reasonable rates and fair service. But in the absence of any effective administrative provision to enforce the statutory standards, the delegated toll power left a large discretion in the grantees to exact from their customers contributions to the capital of the enterprises. This was especially apparent in the second generation of railroad building, when construction usually anticipated rather than responded to traffic demand. Contract clause doctrine recognized that a grant of toll rights delegated to the private grantees a kind of compulsion over others' property such as ordinarily only government might exercise. Hence, unless the statute was very clearly to the contrary, the Supreme Court of the United States construed such grants as subject to the reserved power of the state to require reasonable rates.[54]

The grant of banking franchises, whether involving only the discount or lending function or also that of issuing bank notes, amounted to a delegation of compulsory power over resources allocation in the community. For by commercial loans and by note issues banks increased money or purchasing power rather than merely transferring it as they did when they lent depositors' savings on mortgage. The relation between banks and their borrowers was, of course, voluntary; but insofar as bank loans increased spending and raised prices they exerted force on the whole pattern of community spending, and thus legalization of such banking functions represented a practical delegation of some power of compulsion over the general public. However deficient his economic theory, in his attack on the Second Bank of the United States Benton argued realistically that an issue of broad power was involved in granting that franchise, for such an institution "tends to make and to break fortunes by the flux and reflux of paper."[55]

These grants of banking franchises, toll rights, and eminent domain power were part of a broad pattern of mid–nineteenth-century public policy by which legislation delegated public functions to private groups. Often the law did this simply by encouraging voluntary association; this was largely the way in which we first provided for community hospital, charitable, and educational services. But in an important degree law also delegated powers of legal compulsion, as in this matter of capital mobilization. In every case, of course, the justification had to be the fulfillment of a public purpose. It was natural to the times to engage in this extent of delegation to private effort. Cash was scarce and taxes hard to collect; the Whiskey Rebellion and the house tax riots in Pennsylvania remind us that early nineteenth-century governments had to move with care in employing the public fiscal power directly. Our government institutions were new, untried, inexpertly manned. The variety of practical situations to be dealt with invited all the range of wit and ingenuity we could muster. In such circumstances it was only by broad delegation that a substantial beginning could be made in providing for many framework needs of the community.[56]

Awareness of chronic capital scarcity influenced nineteenth-century public policy in another important respect, besides leading us to use law to assign priorities among objects of current investment. It led also to legal action which in effect assigned priorities among the capital claims or needs of the generations. This bustling century, preoccupied with its immediate opportunities of growth, wrote firmly into statutes and decisions some important preferences—for the promise of the future over commitments to the past, but also for the ambitions of the present over the claims of the future. These legally expressed time preferences produced some of the best and the worst legacies which the nineteenth century left to its successor.

Nineteenth-century public policy expressed several important preferences for keeping open the door to change, as against commitments or equities asserted by the past. The Northwest Ordinance and Congressional practice under the constitutional authority to admit new states established the principle that new states should enter the Union on terms of political equality with the old. National policy implemented this promise with grants of public lands, promotion of internal improvements, and an open door to immigration. Our program thus denied a vested political position to the older states.[57] The *Dartmouth College* case brought corporate franchises within the protection of the contracts clause. State constitutional and legislative policy promptly and unanimously asserted the value placed on opportunity for growth and change by providing that all future charters be subject to amendment or repeal by the legislature. The Supreme Court later put a like premium on the community's control of its evolving situation: Corporate franchises should be strictly construed against the grantees and in favor of the public freedom. The contracts clause did not bar exercise of the police power to regulate conduct under prior corporate grants. The preference accorded new growth had very practical legal expression, for example, in allowing railroad development to override the older claims of turnpikes and river traffic.[58] In the field of credit the adoption of homestead exemptions and other exemptions of debtors' property limited creditors' rights in order to preserve a nucleus of working capital and hence of continued freedom of maneuver for small enterprisers; insolvency and bankruptcy laws expressed analogous policy in a larger theater of operations.[59] Even the dubious case of the protective tariff contributes an item to this pattern of policy. The tariff tended to create static, vested interests; but in its inception it overrode such prior equities in time as commercial and plantation wealth could assert.[60]

Nineteenth-century public policy also declared itself for the ambitious demands of the present over the claims of the future. The century was constantly stimulated by the opportunities it could see close to its hand, tantalized by the lack of working capital to realize its visions, its imagination captured by the incessant pressure of the immediate problems of the physical environment. Charitably appraised, the tariff may offer an instance where present gain from lower prices was sacrificed to a long-range program of building industry. And it is true that distant goals of political and economic balance were commonly brought into debate on transport, land, and credit policy. But characteristically in actual decision there was impatience to make events move then and there, by the handiest means, with scant assessment of future costs.

The development of a railroad network was basic for growth both in community strength and individual opportunity. But we pressed this development at wasteful speed, inviting fraud in aid grants and construction costs, overbuilding, and saddling local governments and farmers with unwisely apportioned and burdensome debt. The third quarter of the century mortgaged the future for present haste in building railroads, and under the contracts clause or under vaguely defined doctrine protective of venture capital the courts rigorously enforced the mortgage.[61] Distrusting the mysterious power of bankers, a dominant opinion yet demanded currency and credit to hasten expansion of markets and increase of land values. We were unwilling to incur the time costs of a slower, more stable finance under central bank discipline; so through most of the century for the sake of present boom we recurrently subjected ourselves to future breakdown. Moreover, we would not set aside resources to provide small farm buyers with low-cost, long-term financing, though this was the logical corollary of our declared public lands policy. Southern opposition to western growth was partly in the background. But, also, in bustling unconcern with "theoretical" matters, imagination generally did not encompass the idea of such a farm credit program. In any case, urgency for rapid settlement tended to work in favor of speculators and large landholders.[62]

Policy or lack of policy in the disposal of public lands provided the most vivid demonstration of the priority which the middle nineteenth century assigned to its immediate growth over the wealth of the future. The vast public domain of 1800 put into the hands of the community an unexampled means for shaping its social environment. Given the hopes and temper of the times, perhaps it was never politically practicable to take any direction other than that we adopted, of the most rapid disposition of the public lands at low returns to the public treasury. In effect, we thus subsidized private decision makers with public capital. Alone among mid-century leaders, John Quincy Adams lamented in this policy a lost opportunity:

The public lands are the richest inheritance ever bestowed by a bountiful Creator upon any national community. All the mines of gold and silver and precious stones on the face or in the bowels of the globe, are in value compared to them, but the dust of the balance. Ages upon ages of continual progressive improvement, physical, moral, political, in the condition of the whole people of this union, were stored up in the possession and disposal of these lands. . . : I had long entertained and cherished the hope that these public lands were among the chosen instruments of Almighty power, . . . of improving the condition of man, by establishing the practical, self-evident truth of the natural equality and brotherhood of all mankind, as the foundation of all human government, and by banishing slavery and war from the earth.

However, though bitterly critical of the disposal policies which he saw wasting this resource, Adams had already recognized that he was opposing overwhelming force:

The thirst of a tiger for blood is the fittest emblem of the rapacity with which the members of all the new states fly at the public lands. The constituents upon whom they depend are all settlers, or tame and careless spectators of the pillage. They are themselves enormous speculators and land-jobbers. It were a vain attempt to resist them here.[63]

This is not the place in which to debate the merits of the great choice which Adams criticized. To his contemporaries it seemed so obvious a public good as to require little deliberation that government should lend any positive aid it could to the immediate exploitation of resources and the freeing of men's energies. A Wisconsin legislative committee expressed the impatient confidence of the times when, in 1842, it urged prompt disposal of public lands held in aid of a state university. The committee conceded that "some think it best to leave [the lands] . . . for ten or twenty years to rise in value, when, as a matter of course, the proceeds would amount to more than if sold at the present time." Apparently ten to twenty years represented the committee's maximum stretch of imagination in defining a long-term policy, and it felt strongly that so long a delay in opening up these lands could not be justified:

. . . [S]hall the early settlers have this privation continued till their children have grown up in ignorance or been educated in other states, merely to give future emigrants a great fund to educate theirs with?

. . . Shall we adopt the anti-republican policy of oppressing the few and the poor, in order to benefit the many and more wealthy who may follow us? We protest against such a policy.

More than local interest would be served by prompt marketing of the lands; there was a national interest in rapid development of the continent:

It is believed that the settlement of the country, which the sale of these lands would encourage, would be a greater public benefit than the enhanced value of the lands, which delay might afford, would be to future immigrants, or to a generation yet unborn. We need the strength of a *present* population to share in the burdens of government, of schools, of roads, and of the public defense in case of war. . . . [Such a course would be] more in accordance with our Republican Institutions—with the wants of a newly settled country, and with the designs of Congress in granting those lands, with a view to encourage the settlement and sale of the public domain, than to hoard up the treasure like a miser, with a view to make a princely fortune for a person or persons yet unborn.

Implicit in the argument was the committee's confidence that rapid marketing of the state's lands would have a desirable multiplier effect, opening many new, active centers of creative energy. The committee's final argument especially revealed the dynamic emphasis behind much of the century's concern for vested rights. Rapid marketing was required in justice to private land speculators. The law had in various ways disfavored the withholding from market of large blocs of land by private speculation; the state could fairly follow no other policy regarding its own property:

. . . [A]s it is a matter of public policy to encourage the settlement of the country, and to effect this object, previous legislation has borne heavily upon the holders of unsettled and unoccupied lands, with a view to compel their sale to actual settlers; can it be said to be good policy to leave our own lands waste and unoccupied? Shall we oppress the speculator who withholds his lands from sale and settlement, for the purpose of enhancing their value, and at the same time withhold our own lands from the market with the same view? Shall we, as a body politic, pursue the same course we condemn in others? [64]

Apart from shifting from public to private owners the benefits of the long-term rise in land values, the nineteenth century assigned another kind of priority to present over future wealth. We would realize the greatest present production we could from the land, though in the contemporary state of the economy this meant throwing away much that a broader future development could use. So farmers burned off great stands of hardwood to clear fields. Lumbermen mined the forests for the most immediately marketable timber, leaving uneconomic islands of residue and cutting without regard to new growth or control of fire hazards. This story is too familiar to require detailing here.[65] For our purpose it is enough to note the presence, in another aspect, of the century's characteristic pattern of time preference in favor of a quick tempo of change so long as it seemed to promise rapid growth.

This essay may appropriately conclude with this attention to the relative priorities which public policy assigned in the first seventy-five years of the century to competing claims of past, present, and future. For it was the gathering sense that both drift and directed movement in time had brought our confident working principles to unexpected outcomes, that led policy to the threshold of new decisions at the end of the century. In consequence we began to redefine the challenge of our social environment.

III

THE BALANCE OF POWER

MEASURED by patterns of legal policy, our "nineteenth century" began with the constitution-making years, 1776–1800, and ended about the time Theodore Roosevelt left the White House (1908). This was the span of fashioning a continental nation. In this length of years legal history moved from prime concern with the political challenge of social environment (1776–1800), into preoccupation with the economic challenge of physical and social circumstance (1800–1870), and then to a renewed political focus upon the general organization of power. True, the post–Civil War generation introduced changes of such order that they made a new nation, with a life qualitatively so different as to demand consideration within its own frame of reference. But these changes were inseparably linked both to the defined objectives and the unforeseen consequences of earlier nineteenth-century policy. The painful effort to understand what was happening to us and the redefinition of policy under the sheer pressure of events formed the necessary conclusion of one chapter of policy in order that we might open another.

Four clusters of fact of primary significance to law marked the emergence of a new order of society in the United States after 1870: (1) big industry, with rising productivity; (2) big finance, with the growth of the *rentier* interest as a subsidiary element; (3) continued large growth in population, accompanied by the relative growth of urban living; (4) increasing interdependence of activities.

Capital put into manufacturing doubled every decade up to 1900 and thereafter increased more slowly. Net national product grew about three times from 1870 to 1900, while population less than doubled, so that national income per capita increased. The percentage of the labor force engaged in nonagricultural work rose from 28 per cent in 1820 to 36 per cent in 1850, to 47 per cent in 1870, to 62 per cent in 1900. Factories became larger, but in the last quarter of the century the larger firms grew at the faster rate. By 1904 manufacturing companies producing over $1 million of value added in manufacturing were less than one per cent of all such concerns, but accounted for about 30 per cent of the total value added by manufacturing. From 1890 to 1904 some 237 corporate consolidations occurred, each involving business of regional or national extent, each capitalized for more than $1 million, representing almost every important field of manufacture. Finance likewise changed character. From 1870 to 1900 around 6 to 7 per cent of a steadily rising national income went into new investment apart from replacement of old facilities. In the second quarter of the century railroad securities dislodged government and bank stocks from their market predominance. In 1867 only 15 industrial shares were traded on the New York Stock Exchange, but by 1896 that Exchange handled a total of 57 million shares, and by 1901, 266 million.

Population changes marched with these events. The most spectacular rate of increase was before the Civil War; population increased elevenfold (from 2,781,000 to 31,443,321) from 1780 to 1869 and then grew less than two and a half times (to 75,994,575) from 1860 to 1900. But throughout the century both relative and absolute increases were such as to reshape the social environment. The main cause of our population increase was a high native birth rate. Immigration was a lesser factor; in 1900 the foreign-born were only about one-seventh of our people. However, the migration of 20 millions of people—about 12 million of them from 1870 to 1900 alone—could not but bring novel issues of social order. More and more people lived in urban areas; but what created the most unusual problems was the rapid growth of metropolitan areas. In 1880 we had 19 cities of 100,000 people or more; in 1900 we had 36; from 1880 to 1900 New York grew from about two to three and a half million, and Chicago from 500,000 to a million and a half; a junior metropolis might develop like Milwaukee, from 71,000 in 1870 to 285,-000 in 1900.

All of this investment, all of these people, moved within a society which found its life more and more dependent on the increase and reliability of key services. Rail and power figures are symbolic. Railway mileage climbed from about 35,000 in 1865 to 74,000 in 1875, to 128,000 in 1885, to about 190,000 by 1900—a 600 per cent growth in 35 years. Mechanical power became a central fact of life, though its character underwent amazing change in short periods. As late as 1870 about half of our industrial power came from water power, but by 1900, 77 per cent of power used in manufacture came from steam engines. Overlapping this growth was the startling increase in use of electricity after the introduction of the transformer (1885); much steam and water power was thence directed into production of electricity so that by 1900 about as much industrial power came from electricity as from steam engines.[1]

The day to day impact of such facts of change put its stamp upon a public opinion little given to theorizing about its situation. Circumstances taught great numbers of people three points of view which greatly affected the demands made on law and the environment in which law operated after 1870. (1) Experience broadened and consolidated longstanding popular expectations of a rising material standard of living at the same time as it turned these expectations more toward industry. (2) But, likewise, experience spread a sharp, new sense of individual helplessness, of the individual's liability to being pushed around by events in this promising society. (3) Partly from these two attitudes, partly from new habits of thought generated by the constant, felt presence of a more organized way of life, we began to develop a new disposition of calculation. There was a new inclination to think in matter-of-fact terms about cause and effect in social relations and to cast up balance sheets of profit and loss in matters of community-wide effect.

James Bryce saw at work in the United States of the eighties a pattern of values born of the implicit teachings of science and technology, but with profound effect upon legal policy:

New causes are at work in the world tending not only to lengthen the arms of government, but to make its touch quicker and firmer. . . . Modern civilization, in becoming more complex and refined, has become more exacting. It discerns more benefits which the organized power of government can secure, and grows more anxious to attain them. Men live fast, and are impatient of the slow working of natural laws. The triumphs of physical science have enlarged their desires for comfort, and shown them how many things may be accomplished by the application of collective skill and large funds which are beyond the reach of individual effort. Still greater has been the influence of a quickened moral sensitiveness and philanthropic sympathy. The sight of preventible evil is painful, and is felt as a reproach. . . .[2]

Faith in our ability to master environment, especially to the end of rising productivity, was deep bred; but the industrial revolution after the Civil War taught this faith in new form with new urgency both to native-born and to immigrants.

However, great expectations made frustration the more bitter. Big industry, big finance, big cities, big markets overshadowed individual lives. The people of the new metropolis found their disappointment hardest to express, for they lacked a justifying tradition of urban protest. Jacob Riis put the isolation of the immigrant into the accusing description of "How the Other Half Lives." The bewildered anger and searching of jobless native workers was taken out in the railroad riots of 1877, in the groping for a program by the short-lived, amorphous Knights of Labor (1870–1890), and in the pitiful "petition in boots" of Coxey's army (1894). Equally bewildered and angry as they struggled in the market net, the farmers yet had a tradition of agrarian politics to lend their protest more righteous confidence. The trumpets of the Grange and the Farmers' Alliance sounded their voice. But there remained a core of inarticulate feeling, captured by Hamlin Garland, whose midwest stories Howells found

full of the gaunt, grim, sordid, pathetic, ferocious figures, whom our satirists find so easy to caricature as Hayseeds, and whose blind groping for fairer conditions is so grotesque to the newspapers and so menacing to the politicians. They feel that something is wrong, and they know that the wrong is not theirs. The type . . . is not pretty; it is ugly and often ridiculous; but it is heart-breaking in its rude despair.[3]

We must read between the lines of the statute books and the court opinions to find the early symbols of a new sense of calculation that was entering men's consideration of public policy. It was a matter-of-fact approach to problems, a bent toward the greater rationalization of social operations, which by its nature was more often implied in prosaic instances than it was embodied in polemic. It appeared chiefly in patterns of legislation, for example, in increasing provision to collect and publish economic and social statistics, or in statutes which created rudimentary budgeting procedures. Lacking attitude surveys for the late nineteenth century, we obtain some rough equivalent when we note that a stout 500-page volume on political economy became a best seller, went through over 100 editions, and by 1906 was read by perhaps six million people. Peddled in railway coaches by candy "butchers" along with the paperback joke books and thrillers of the day, Henry George's *Progress and Poverty* (1879) evidently responded to some pervasive, deep-felt need to probe and grasp for more understanding of cause and effect in social relations.[4]

These primary and derivative facts of life and attitudes were not without relation to the public policy written into law in the first three-quarters of the century. On the other hand, our situation at the end of the century, so far as these facts define it, was certainly not the product of calculation. Policy made by drift and default bulked larger than deliberated decision in forming the century's final legacy to its successor.

The release-of-energy principle contributed to the currents of 1870–1908 mainly by providing a range of flexible contract and association devices, notably the corporation and the procedures of large-scale finance. Two elements of drift and default gave unexpected direction and effect to this release of energy. Contract and free private association suggest relations entered voluntarily; the compulsion involved is ostensibly only that to which persons have given some initial consent. The first unforeseen factor that entered the play of the release-of-energy principle was the enormous expansion of practical compulsion imposed on strangers to contracts or associations, as commercial and industrial corporations and investment bankers reached out to occupy the multi-state markets whose availability the law had guaranteed. Economic growth tied the lives of an increasing proportion of people to the market and the division of labor; they were either wage or salary earners, or small producers or traders in specialized ranges of goods or services. Theoretically buyers consent to the practical compulsions of the market in which they buy; if they do not consent, they stay out. But men who find their whole livelihood in the market are too vulnerable to stay out. An outstanding recognition of this simple but slowly learned truth was the legislation which limited or abolished the employer's defense of assumption of risk in industrial accident cases. To balance the reach for broader trade areas on the one hand, and the individual's access to new markets on the other, became of manifest concern to the late nineteenth-century courts as they dealt with covenants by the seller of a business not to compete with his buyer. It was more than coincidence that the end of the nineteenth century, which produced the definitive victory of a market-oriented way of life, also produced an emerging pattern of law dealing with obstruction of access to markets. Intimidation by violence, threats of harassing litigation, slander of goods, bogus competition, interference with contract relations, boycotts, and exclusive dealing arrangements barring the door to trade opportunities took on critical meaning when all livelihood turned upon participation in trading or the availability of employment.[5]

We had to learn a second major lesson about our release-of-energy principle. During the first half of the century we expressed that principle chiefly through contract. But sound doctrine for so fundamental a community concern as the organization of power requires built-in points of view and procedures to take account of all important values in the situation. Contract was inherently too limited an institution to serve this need. Its nature was to express and serve the immediate interests of bargaining parties; indeed, this restricted focus upon the contractor's ambitions was what made contract socially useful as the prime legal device to multiply the release of individual or group energies. Moreover, as a matter of law private individuals or groups were held quite strictly to their roles as private contractors or property owners. A litigant who claimed to vindicate a public interest might generally find standing in court only if he could show that his suit would likewise protect his special interest. Conversely, if a broad public policy came in issue in a private lawsuit—as in a question of the constitutionality or interpretation of a statute—there was little the public authorities might do to intervene, to speak directly on behalf of the public program. Again, pursuit of profit not only justified doing ordinary competitive damage to a market rival, but was a business firm's whole legal excuse for being. When Henry Ford would have cut car prices for the declared purpose of spreading employment and wealth, the Michigan court, in terms which carry the tone of the late nineteenth century, declared this not a proper corporate policy: "A business corporation is organized and carried on primarily for the profit of the stockholders . . . [I]t is not within the lawful powers of a board of directors to shape and conduct the affairs of a corporation for the merely incidental benefit of shareholders and for the primary purpose of benefiting others. . . ." [6]

The cautious sense that contract alone was not a sufficient organizing principle for society never quite deserted us. Always the courts held onto a residual power to refuse enforcement to contracts which they found to offend public policy. From the Taney years the Supreme Court never deviated from the ruling that the contracts clause did not prevent the operation of state police power upon existing agreements. These reservations were significant. However, not until events set their current after 1870 were legislatures or courts pressed to make broad use of the authority so reserved.

Moreover, the very care with which we reserved power to "police" enforcement of contracts or behavior in which contracts might be involved expressed a dangerous limit on imagination. Implicit here was the notion that the important thing was to deal with the positive social harms that men might willfully do. But the most serious damage that preoccupation with contract wrought in important areas of our life was done not through willfulness but through indifference or lack of power in fact. Matters like public health which affected everyone or at least broad, substantial parts of the population were by reason of their very pervasive nature of no such particularized meaning as would make them the objects of contractors' concern. Matters which critically concerned people of the future, but which had little save a moral claim on the interests of a present generation would not become subjects of contract, nor was there practical incentive to weigh them in present contract arrangements. Our nineteenth-century economists reflected this engrossing concern with exchange value when they equated economics with the study of market equilibria. Our law reflected this when it equated "value" with "market value," as in eminent domain. Even Herbert Spencer was appalled at the "exclusive devotion to work" which he found in the United States of 1882; this apostle of the market felt impelled to caution us that a broader calculus of social values than the market place offered was imperative to fulfill life's possibilities and that while "the primary use of work is that of supplying the materials and aids to living completely; and . . . any other uses of work are secondary," nevertheless, "in men's conceptions the secondary has in great measure usurped the place of the primary." [7]

The conservation of natural resources was a conspicuous social value, which suffered perhaps as much from the indifference as from the deliberate or reckless waste of contractors. Moreover, there were overhead costs of a division-of-labor, market-oriented society, which contractors could not cover in their agreements even had they conceived of the idea. Such, for example, was the cost of a major downswing in the business cycle. With characteristic insight Tocqueville had seen as early as the 1830's the beginnings of this vulnerability of a contract-focused society:

The Americans make immense progress in productive industry, because they all devote themselves to it at once; and for this same reason they are exposed to unexpected and formidable embarrassments. As they are all engaged in commerce, their commercial affairs are affected by such various and complex causes that it is impossible to foresee what difficulties may arise. As they are all more or less engaged in productive industry, at the least shock given to business all private fortunes are put in jeopardy at the same time, and the state is shaken. I believe that the return of these commercial panics is an endemic disease of the democratic nations of our age. It may be rendered less dangerous, but it cannot be cured, because it does not originate in accidental circumstances, but in the temperament of these nations. [8]

However, we had thought simple provision for release of men's energies not enough; we had sought also to control environment, positively to enlarge men's range of practical choices. Thus we used law to guarantee freedom of maneuver within multi-state and state-wide markets. This was one area where deliberate policy worked out substantially according to plan. There was no end to the ingenuity or persistence of special or local interests in seeking to fence off markets for themselves. But this was only more of a familiar story, early anticipated. The growth of industrial investment and productivity through the end of the century attested that the broad markets were in fact kept open.[9] Of course, the law merely guaranteed the framework of opportunity; it was science, technology, the invention of financial procedures, and the massing of capital which supplied the dynamic force to occupy these broad areas of economic maneuver. Insofar as there were great, unforeseen consequences from our legal guarantees of broad markets, these flowed from the way in which that policy gave play to turbulent currents of capital growth.

Net capital accumulation went on after 1870 at a steady but relatively modest rate. It was the distribution rather than the over-all rate of capital accumulation which reshaped society. This distribution concentrated unprecedented power of decision in private hands, first in the railroads, then in heavy industry and in investment banking houses and life insurance companies. In part this was the product of deliberate public policy; directly and indirectly we used the compulsion of law to promote capital mobilization in ways which the previous essay discussed. But there is little evidence that anyone foresaw or intended the kind and extent of concentration of capital which ensued. Default and drift in legal policy contributed materially to this development.

The economic historians do not tell us much about the particular patterns of capital growth in the late nineteenth century. Thus it seems highly probable that the defects of our public lands policy had important, if indirect, effect on the directions which capital accumulation took; but there is as yet scant evidence as to just what happened. The bargain by which states holding large western land claims relinquished these to the central government as a condition of securing adherence of the landless states to the Union was a decision of great significance for the relation of public land policy to capital formation. This step probably prevented the early creation of great, concentrated private land holdings out of public lands. By the time the central government began to make the bulk of its large-scale grants, the country's growth had set firmly in the pattern of population increase and westward movement which meant that market speculation in land rather than landlordism seemed the obvious way to realize on its value. But the evidence is still scanty and inconclusive as to the money that was made out of marketing public land and where the money came to rest.

It seems doubtful that great, unexpected windfalls came to the railroads from their aid land grants. These contributed materially to meeting the costs of railroad construction, as they were intended to, and some roads sold land very advantageously; but the pressing financial needs of the roads generally led to rapid sale of the lands at rather ordinary prices. On the other hand, the low price which the government set on its land probably had material effect in building up investment capital; lenders could exact and obtain high returns on good security from necessitous settlers, as the growth of population and settlers' improvements built up land values above the low government price. Perhaps the most important effect which the deficiencies of public land policy had upon the direction of capital accumulation arose out of the lack of any proper system of land classification. Throughout most of the century the national and state governments sold their land with no adequate regard to the special resources in soils, minerals, or timber which might make particular tracts of extraordinary value. Many of the first generation of land speculators, it seems, made little money or actually suffered net losses because they lacked the capital to hold on for the long-term rise in value of such specially rich tracts. But the gains were high for those who could hold on or for the second generation of land investors; and from this source arose an important new branch of *rentier* wealth for investment in industry as well as agriculture. Wisconsin history furnishes some evidence of the scale of such long-term gains where they could be achieved. The state took little time to sell the 240,000 acres which the federal government gave it for its agricultural college, and realized about $300,000 on some good land. Ezra Cornell used New York's Morrill Act land scrip to locate about 500,000 acres of pine lands in Wisconsin on behalf of Cornell University. Sales of this land were stretched beyond 1893 for a net realization of about $5 million.[10]

The circumstances that plunged us into a great Civil War pressed the federal government into a fiscal role which it might otherwise never have assumed, with great, unforeseen consequences for capital concentration. War contracts fostered large-scale production, and their proceeds put large amounts of capital into entrepreneurs' hands. Legal direction of the flow of capital was implicit in the practical realities of big government contracting: there was power to choose favorites; sales taxes meant that integrated producers could make more money because they eliminated separate taxable stages of production.

More important in scale and long-range effect was the central government's flotation of over two and a half billion dollars of bonds and its issue of $450 million of paper money not redeemable in specie. Bought with depreciated paper money and paid off finally in gold, the $1,800 million of wartime bonds which the federal government redeemed from 1866 to 1893 amounted to a capital subsidy to their holders, supplied out of taxes on consumers. Originally the debt was widely owned. But after the completion of refunding in 1880 official estimates indicated that over 82 per cent of it was held in amounts of $10,000 or more. The tax-derived payments on the debt thus went mainly to swell already concentrated wealth. While this tendency developed, the handling of the debt represented the single largest impact of federal fiscal policy; from 1866 to 1879 average annual expenditure on the debt was just short of $150 million, compared with average total expenditures for other federal purposes of $192.5 million.

Resumption of specie payments on the federal government's paper money (1875–1879) spelled a further tax-supported subsidy to creditors, whose debtors must now pay back in money of higher purchasing power than that they had borrowed. Moreover, the unredeemed wartime bonds became the basis for note issues by the new national banks; the federal tax power supporting the bonds thus enlarged the scope of available credit for business. On the other hand, the reliance on borrowing and printing money to finance the Civil War meant that there had not been a heavy tax load on industry or entrepreneurs in the war years; the income tax of 1861–1872 produced about 20 per cent of federal revenue over that time; the excise taxes which brought in the bulk of tax revenue fell mainly on consumers. Against this pattern of events it was no accident that, next to railroad regulation, legal policy toward money and finance provided the focus of political agitation from 1870 through 1893. The sharp reactions of the Greenback movement and Bryan's silver campaign evidenced the felt compulsion of law in the moulding of social environment.[11]

A third unforeseen factor with which drift and default of legal policy played in for great consequences after 1870 was the tendency of large-scale economic operations to breed still larger-scale operations. Our vision of wider areas for economic maneuver, our urgent sense of need to mobilize capital, had not anticipated the accelerating momentum with which the forces so mobilized and released would roll forward. Optimistic as we were at mid-century about our "inexhaustible" natural resources and the "startling magnitude" of the growth in manufactures, policy from 1870 to 1890 showed little realistic appreciation of the scale of retained earnings in strategic industry or the extent of enforced and voluntary savings collected from the people into investment banking coffers and life insurance.

The total net assets of the Standard Oil combination went from $72 million in 1883 to $143 million in 1895, to $359 million in 1906; total annual net earnings, which were never less than 10 per cent of total net assets in any of these years, averaged over 14 per cent between 1883 and 1895 and probably over 24 per cent between 1896 and 1906. Standard Oil dividends were always substantial, but stayed within a small circle of recipients; Mr. John D. Rockefeller, for example, received in dividends between $15 and $20 million from 1885 to 1890, and between $20 and $27 million from 1891 to 1896. With a steel business capitalized at $700,-000 in 1873, Andrew Carnegie and his associates earned $40 million in the 20 years from 1873 to 1892; from 1890 to 1900 annual profits increased from $5,400,000 to $40 million, and the company's annual steel production from 322,000 to 3 million tons. At the end of the span of years which in policy pattern form the "nineteenth century," the rise of the Ford Motor Company provided another spectacular example of capital growth born of mass markets. From 1903 to March 1, 1913 (at the birth of the federal income tax amendment), the founders brought an original cash investment of $28,000 to $22 million after having paid dividends of $15 million; retained earnings financed the entire development of plant; in the five years before March 1, 1913, profits averaged 118 per cent annually on investment, and in 1912 profits were over 132 per cent. The assets of the 11 largest life insurance companies reporting to New York state authorities increased from an already impressive total of $328 million in 1881 to $771 million in 1893, to $2,393 million in 1907, an increase just short of 600 per cent over the whole span of years; by 1904 Mutual Life, New York Life, and the Equitable Society overshadowed the industry with total assets of over $1,100 million. From 1880 past the 1912 investigation of the House Committee on Banking and Currency, half a dozen investment banking houses in the East grew to dominate the finance of business and largely affected the use of insurance company assets. Sizable as were the immediate resources of the investment bankers, their greatest significance was in the skill with which they employed the leverage of their capital at strategic points. J. P. Morgan & Company, the National City Bank, and the First National Bank showed total assets in 1912 of $632 million; also, they had financial affiliations which increased their minimum working resources to $2,104 million; thus in 1910 a Morgan investment of $3 million in Equitable Life Assurance Society stock gave that house control of the insurance

company's $504 million of assets; partners in the three leading invest-
ment banking concerns in 1912 held 341 directorships in 112 corporations
of a combined capitalization over $22 billion.[12]

The years of capital growth and concentration after the Civil War
were our most influential generation of laissez faire, if we ever had one.
The law provided an open field (assured broad markets), legal instruments (the corporation and manifold tools of contract, especially the
devices of corporate finance), legal subsidies (grants of land and public
credit, and currency inflation and deflation), and then substantially stood
aside. Except for the struggling Interstate Commerce Commission (1887),
no legal agency policed the critical marketing practices or financial
standards. There was not even any federal or state agency for systematic
study of the interplay of the law's action or inaction with the new
industrial and financial forces. Perhaps the most important contribution
which the law's omission made to the concentration of capital was the
narrow use of the tax power. After the Civil War income tax ended in
1872, except for the abortive income tax of 1894, tax law not only laid
no hand upon capital concentration, but practically promoted it; there
were no general income, gift, or inheritance taxes; the closest analogy
to a corporation income tax was state levies on the receipts of railroads
and other utilities, which, like the tariff and other excises and the real
estate property tax, fell mainly on ultimate consumers or small businessmen and farmers. Thus industry and finance could operate within a
framework of social order paid for by other people. The pressure of
public fiscal policy on economic activity in the years 1870–1914, Schumpeter observes, was "so light as to justify exclusion from the general
analysis of the determining factors of the economic process." [13]

On the present evidence it is hard to reach a satisfying judgment as
to how much calculation and how much default of legal policy contributed
to the concentration of capital. The generation after the Civil War did
not lack actors to occupy the forestage of events; it may be easy to
exaggerate their roles. There was melodrama, chiefly from the railroad
gamblers and empire builders. Ruthless, hard-driving planning and execution of a cooler sort created other power centers, like Standard Oil
or the Morgan house. Both swashbucklers and men of cool reckoning
could sometimes manipulate law for their ends; once they secured the
railroad aid grants and the protective tariff, from the eighties on their
ends tended chiefly toward being let alone.

But the predominant values and attitudes of the people never challenged the masters of industry and finance on the key point of capital

concentration during the years which consolidated the new pattern of power. Thus these men never had to test their capacity to form public policy on the critical issue. Minority parties and pamphleteers cried against plutocracy. But they presented the problem of the domestic balance of power in terms too vague to make a rallying philosophy of radical impact. The actual battles on which major effort centered in these years were fought on quite restricted questions, compared with the reach and depth of structural change that capital concentration was bringing. Control of railroads focused on the marginal reasonableness and equality of rates and service, and the farmers' fervor died away remarkably with easier times. Greenbackers and Silverites pinned their faith on manipulating one instrument of social control; they found support chiefly in emotions raised in hard times rather than in any broad popular concern with social organization. Henry George won wide attention for a general economic analysis which, however, he would implement with a single control device that touched only the fringes of the new kinds of power. Nothing more stamped the late nineteenth century in historic stereotype for its laissez faire philosophy than the court decisions which, in the name of freedom of contract, overthrew legislation limiting hours of work and regulating terms of pay and conditions of labor. These were matters of great concern both from an economic and a humane standpoint. But, again, they did not go to the heart of the new organization of power in the community; indeed, such legislation implicitly recognized that life had been thrown into a wholly novel frame of social reference and sought simply to work out more decent accommodations to it.

At least as much as men's ambitions, what reshaped this society in the span of 1870–1900 was a pace of change which outran men's imagination, philosophy, and administrative competence. We neither realized nor had the capacity to affect our transformation until we were committed. There was operating in this generation a cumulative impact of events like the lines of force or fields of attraction which Henry Adams seized on about this time to explain the direction of history.

One striking indication how little contemporary opinion comprehended the significance of the movement of capital was the scant attention given the idea of the progressive income tax. From the early seventies minority parties and polemicists included the income tax in their programs. But they did not stress it much as a means to affect concentration of capital; proponents emphasized the limited objective of a more equitable sharing of the costs of government; the opposition rarely saw the issue as an attack on capital concentration, but complained that an income tax would burden production and penalize efficiency while encouraging extravagant public expenditure.[14]

Prevailing popular values generally gave high status to profit-making and the role of the energetic entrepreneur. The striking industrial advances after 1850 confirmed a longstanding faith that rising productivity was the key to a better general life and strengthened a traditional belief that change would be for the better. Our habits of thought and skill assigned status to Yankee handiness at the work bench; our interest, after the constitution-making generation, had long been turned away from social arrangements. The relative indifference of popular opinion toward the planning of social policy was underwritten by the tendency of both classical and Marxist economists of the nineteenth century to seek out deterministic "laws" controlling economic behavior beyond the power of individual wills. Mr. Dooley's summary of Theodore Roosevelt's first message to Congress summed up a great deal in our working philosophy, not only for the late nineteenth century but for the middle twentieth, too. We distrusted great power in private hands; but, also, we were not sure how much we could do about it, and we did not want to upset our applecarts:

Iv all th' gr-reat evils now threatenin' th' body politic and th' pollytical bodies, these crool organizations an' combinations iv capital is perhaps th' best example iv what upright an' arnest businessmen can do whin they are let alone. They cannot be stamped out be laws or th' decisions iv coorts, or hos-tile ligislachion which is too frindly. Their desthruction cannot be accomplished be dimagogues.

Th' thrusts are heejous monsthers built up be th' inlightened intherprise iv th' men that have done so much to advance pro-gress in our beloved counthry. On wan hand I wud stamp thim undher fut; on th' other hand not so fast.[15]

That events ran away with us after 1870 is a fact which leaves little present relevance in debating whether it was good or bad that things happened so. These years did, however, provide a lesson in the practical importance of studied attention to organization in a society marked by high interdependence and an accelerating tempo of change. As we began to take stock of our end-of-century situation under the sheer pressure of events, we thus began to reassign emphasis among the challenges we faced. The challenge of the physical environment which had so gripped our imagination at the start of the nineteenth century gave way to preoccupation with the challenge of social environment, now seen more in the terms of the political organization of power which had been our concern from 1776 to 1800. Corollary to this, deriving from a fresh sense of the constraint of our radically changed social situation, we began to use law with growing consciousness of a need to meet the challenge of the personal environment, set by individuals' emotional response to circumstance. In all of this there was a new emphasis on social contriving which had significance for legal history, for it spelled a point of view which naturally involved more self-conscious resort to law as the expression of values.

Though late nineteenth-century public policy did not effectively define the problem posed by shifts in the distribution of power within the community, it did make significant turns in direction of emphasis.

The familiar release-of-energy principle responded to our situation after 1870 through the freedom which law gave for association. Men and women joined in large, staffed and disciplined program groups such as our public life had not seen before—the Grange (1867), the Farmers' Alliance (1874, 1887), the Knights of Labor (1869), the American Federation of Labor (1881), the Grand Army of the Republic (1866), the American Woman Suffrage Association and the National Woman Suffrage Association (1869), the American Association of the Red Cross (1881), the General Federation of Women's Clubs (1890), the Women's Christian Temperance Union (1874), the Anti-Saloon League (1893), the National Civil Service Reform League (1881), the political and fraternal organizations of the foreign-born, among whom "Knights and Orders . . . flourished in a bewildering Gothic variety." Trade associations and business lobby groups took more formal shape in these years, too; the United States Brewers Association, for example, dates from 1862, the National Potters Association organized in 1875, the Stove Founders National Defense Association in 1886, the National Association of Manufacturers in 1895.[16]

That entrepreneurs should close ranks was natural to the self-conscious drive of interest inherent in their role. But such an array of secular groups of large membership, organized around modest economic interests or social or civic purposes or for the advancement of personal status, represented unaccustomed thrusts of desire and fear in the society. Their development reflected pervasive unease and dissatisfaction with emerging patterns of power and the lack of defined policy toward emerging issues. A radical restructuring of human relations was under way in which our unplanned course followed the line of Calhoun's foresight of thirty years before—"Power [could] only be resisted by power —and tendency by tendency." The emotion with which people gave their allegiance to these associations testified, however, that they sought more than a balance of power; through these groups they sought status, self-respect, and some command of their circumstances as individuals. Exercising their freedom to enlist with others and using law positively to mobilize group power in behalf of individual status, people groped toward policy expressing what they felt as a basic truth of civilized existence. It was a proposition which assumed especially poignant meaning in the kind of a society we were becoming. The anthropologist suggests part of the framework within which to view this resort to association:

We are prone to think of environment in terms of natural phenomena such as temperature, terrain or available food supply, factors which inevitably vary with the time and place. Although these things are reflected in the individual's experience and through this in his personality, they seem to be of rather minor importance in personality formation. Between the natural environment and the individual there is always interposed a human environment which is vastly more significant. This human environment consists of an organized group of other individuals, that is, a society, and of a particular way of life which is characteristic of this group, that is, a culture. It is the individual's interaction with these which is responsible for the formation of most of his behavior patterns, even his deep-seated emotional responses. . . . Unpleasant as the realization may be to egotists, very few individuals can be considered as more than incidents in the life histories of the societies to which they belong. Our species long ago reached the point where organized groups rather than their individual members became the functional units in its struggle for survival. . . .[17]

But law was also part of the frame of reference in this society and culture —in the form of the centuries-old Western tradition of constitutionalism. The survival of the group had meaning only as the condition of individuality; our Declaration had been for "all men"; our Bill of Rights stood to the end that "no person" be deprived of respect as an individual.

Freedom of private association was a value built sturdily into our habits of life. This was the fact that gave vitality to constitutional declarations of rights of assembly and petition. It was the fact which lay back of our consistent, practical expansion of the chartering of business corporations through all the swirl of Jacksonian debate. By the eighties the prevalence of general incorporation laws expressed a policy so accepted as to amount to constitutional principle: Men should enjoy the privilege of incorporating for their ordinary purposes at their own initiative, while the state played generally a passive, ministerial role, implementing their decisions.[18]

Thus there was no sustained effort to curb by law the unusual extent of group action and agitation after 1870. The exceptions only underlined the general acceptance of individual expression through group voices. Strange accents, talking proletarian revolt, aroused fears which the Haymarket bomb exploded; there followed a criminal conspiracy trial in Illinois, which Altgeld's pardons and sober later opinion pronounced unjust and based in effect on a doctrine of guilt by association which the main lines of nineteenth-century policy disavowed; individuals were not to be proscribed as members of a class or because they had joined themselves to an identified group. Indeed, the law recognized an affirmative obligation to protect private organizations, and there were successful nineteenth-century prosecutions for riot against those who organized violence against unpopular groups. In 1896 Republican campaigners depicted the fight against Bryan as a rally at the ballot box to suppress by political process the growth of farmer-labor-inspired class war; but after emotion sank, cooler judgment was that the fight had still been within the family—nonetheless bitter, perhaps more bitter, for all of that, but yet not presenting issues of irreconcilable group division. Labor conflict produced the broadest area of restraint on private group activity toward the end of the century. From the eighties on state courts abused their equity powers to restrict strikes, picketing, and boycotts, often by *ex parte* injunction; in 1895 the United States Supreme Court sustained an injunction against the Pullman strikers on the ground of interference with the mails, in the most dramatic episode in a growing use of the injunction by federal courts in labor disputes. In one important area judge-made law thus set substantial limits on group action, relaxed only through legislation in the 1930's. On the other hand, even where trade unions were involved, the nineteenth-century courts generally favored private association by quite consistent refusal to interfere in the internal affairs of private organizations. Private groups were thus accorded a broad leeway to fix and enforce rules of conduct for their members, to determine group programs and enforce members' loyalty to these, and to set professional or trade standards which affected the public as well as their own membership. Further, in the last quarter of the century legislation began explicitly to delegate regulation of practice in some areas to private societies of artisans or professional men, and often to provide that such private groups might nominate or recommend the appointment of the public officials in charge of their regulation. With remarkable acquiescence we moved in this closing quarter of the century into an era of organized group expression of interests.[19]

It now took more deliberate, concerted effort than it once did to create conditions of some practical freedom of choice for ordinary people. Extended resort to association declared our consciousness of this fact. For all the limitations of our policy, we showed this, also, in new uses of law to shape the social environment. Concern with the general organization of power had once before held our prime attention. Then, in the span of 1776–1800, we saw the problem of enlarging private liberty in terms of curbing arbitrary official power, especially executive power. As we focused anew in the seventies upon the organization of power, our prime concern was almost wholly with the pressure of private force upon individual liberty, whether this force was exercised within or outside of government. As was natural to the preoccupation of the times, the kinds of imbalance of private power which worried us were almost always economic-based and of significance primarily with regard to men's positions in the market.

The hard-paced, rough-and-tumble, trial-and-error development of the law of public utility regulation between 1870 and 1908 was our first and principal effort of the time to redress the domestic balance of power. Mr. Chief Justice Waite stressed the central fact about which this history turned when he characterized the Chicago grain elevators whose regulation the Court upheld in Munn v. Illinois: "They stand, to use again the language of their counsel, in the very 'gateway of commerce,' and take toll from all who pass." [20]

In less than one generation we had developed a society highly vulnerable at key points through which essential production or services were channelled. Railroads were the most obvious strategic institution with their 600 per cent increase in mileage from 1865 to 1900; the economy was also deeply involved with auxiliary transport and handling services —not only warehouses, but also express companies, pipelines, wharves, river improvement and booming companies, the telegraph, commodity exchanges, and stockyards. There were other operations as vital to the new ways of community living. Private waterworks increased from 50 in 1850 to 195 in 1875, to nearly 1,500 in 1896; gasworks went from 30 in 1849 to 390 in 1869, numbered over 700 by 1890, and nearly 1,300 by 1910; from the first two central electric power stations of 1882, the number went to 3,600 by 1902 and to 4,700 by 1907; there were nine commercially operated electric street railways in this country in 1885, 789 by 1890, 987 by 1902, and 1,260 in 1912; Bell system telephone stations went from 155,000 in 1885 to 835,000 in 1900, and to 3,900,000 by 1910.[21]

Our first decision was to rely on competition to enforce responsibility in some of these new areas of vital service—in effect, to hope that the release-of-energy principle would produce regulation as a useful by-product. Thus, for a time, Wisconsin farmers were so optimistic as to hope that, if the federal government would foot the bill, improved water transport by the Mississippi or even a Great Lakes Seaway would curb the railroads' arrogance.[22] The Granger legislation of the seventies and the supporting decision in *Munn* v. *Illinois* represented a major turn in policy, away from this principle to positive legal controls. Competition in railroading fostered oppressive rates at points beyond its reach. In any case, both the economics of transport and the push of private ambition steadily advanced the trend of railroad consolidation to contract the area of competition. Wisconsin experience was typical; there were recurrent flurries of legislative opposition to consolidation, followed by acceptance of it as a fact which spelled the need of regulation of rates and service. Competition as the regulator of public utilities lasted as a policy somewhat longer in the field of local services, but there, too, it was generally put aside toward the end of the century.[23]

Implicit in the broadening pattern of the statute books and in the holdings of the cases which sustained an extending reach of regulation after 1875 was a simpler policy than the leading opinions would concede. The tortuous course of doctrinal combat from Field's dissent in *Munn* v. *Illinois* to the clean sweep for simplicity made in *Nebbia* v. *New York* is too familiar to recite. In any case, our concern is more with defining working principle. The working principle was plain enough from what we did: We recognized that life together now depended on critical channels of energy flow, indispensable points of communication of data and impulse, sustaining functions for complicated networks of expectation and reliance. Organization rather than gadgets supplies the vitality of any society; but with us organization had become more than a basic assumption of social life, it was the essence of our peculiar multiplication of energy. In characteristic, unphilosophical fashion, by developing the public utility concept in the late nineteenth century, we acknowledged the heightened social value of organization as a social resource and declared that we would by law hold accountable for the public interest those who stood at strategic points in the organizational network.[24]

The law of public utilities recognized the existence of key points in social organization. The development of capital concentration after the Civil War presented a more generalized problem in the balance of power than this; legal policy slowly indicated growing awareness of the fact. Our inheritance from the Parliamentary Revolution included the idea of private property as a system of legally guaranteed dispersion of decision-making power through the community. The Commercial Revolution had tied this institution of private property to the market and made the market the typical arena of expression for these many semiautonomous centers of decision. One of the doctrines with which English law bulwarked the newly conceived private property was a policy restrictive of Crown grants of monopoly. This was reflected in the amendment which several states proposed to include in the Bill of Rights of our Federal Constitution, banning statutory grants of monopoly. Mingled fear of government-fostered monopoly and undue concentration of private power supplied much of the dynamics of the Jacksonian attack on the Second Bank of the United States and continued as an important thread in the Greenback and Free Silver battles against a government policy of deflation after the war. But this all centered on fear that special interests might capture the positive power of government and use it to upset the balance of power in the market. What was new in the generation of the seventies, we slowly realized, was the threat to market balance from private concentration of capital, proceeding under the spur of invention in technology and in methods of finance and distribution within the permissive framework of our release-of-energy principle.

We were slow to see that in the context of postwar organizational and technical invention released market energy was spinning into gathering centers of growth which could destroy the market as an institution for dispersion of power. The incredibly rapid development of the problem is part of the nineteenth-century story; its definition begins, haltingly, in the eighties; but if we measure the existence of a policy by working reality, the history here really belongs to the twentieth century.

Definition of problem and policy began in the courts. That this was so was significant of the way in which events outran our imagination and energies. Mr. Chief Justice Ryan led the Wisconsin court into a dramatic but isolated effort at railroad regulation through resort to the visitatorial powers of equity judges over corporations. Otherwise, once we set about regulating the roads, we quickly recognized that the problem was of a scope and difficulty which called for legislative and executive handling. Turning as they did on the legislature's traditional control of fiscal policy, the tariff and the money questions always centered in legislation. But to cope with these great, specific issues seemed to exhaust our nineteenth-century resources in public debate. Though both popular and professional opinion accepted the market as an institution practically of constitutional status and function, for thirty critical years we left the immense problem of maintaining the vitality of this institution to the initiative, pocket-books, and courage of individual litigants.[25]

The courts grappled with the problem of preserving the market in two types of decisions. Late nineteenth-century tort law began to develop doctrine dealing with protection of entrepreneurs' access to the market, as against various specific competitive wrongs—boycott, harassing litigation, slander of goods, predatory price cutting, and the like. The broader issue was presented in about a score of reported cases between 1848 and 1890 dealing with agreements directly in restraint of trade, other than conventional contracts made in connection with the sale of a business or the end of an employment. The decisions tended toward strictness; three-quarters of them found the questioned agreements to be illegal. However, the opinions spelled out no unified doctrine. So acute a reader as Circuit Judge William Howard Taft thought that the pre-1890 decisions showed that at common law only restraints ancillary to sale of a business or termination of an employment might be justified. But others have found this a dubious interpretation of the cases and discover at least three different rules in them: that all restrictive, non-ancillary agreements among persons on the same level of trade were illegal *per se;* that, regardless of its effect on competition among the contractors, an agreement was illegal only if it substantially affected competition in some broad market; that any restrictive agreement was presumptively valid, and would be denied effect only if found unreasonable, under criteria which the decisions left conveniently vague.[26]

From the retrospect of the 1950's, the Sherman Act of 1890 looks as if it must have been a turning point of great moment in nineteenth-century policy. But there was a curiously tepid quality to this declaration, as it occurred; the Sherman Act has more importance to us than it seems to have had to its contemporaries. It was only in our century that executive initiative and judicial inventiveness gave body and thrust to the federal government's responsibility for maintaining the market as an institution.

Presidential messages warned that the "trusts" were a threat, but no real Presidential pressure lay back of the Sherman Act. There is no evidence that anti-trust planks in the major party platforms of the time responded to ardent opinion; there was no contemporary flood of petitions, no popular lobby for a federal anti-trust statute, and the current newspapers paid little attention to the Congressional maneuvers and debates out of which the act emerged. Most of the Congressional discussion dealt with other and more specific bills than that which passed;

indeed, apart from providing a useful token of concern for the farmers, lest industry abuse the price leeway which the protective tariff gave it, the practical occasion for the Sherman Act may have been largely that its generalities relieved Congressmen of the embarrassments of more specific proposals then pressed on them. Whatever some of the Congressional debaters thought to the contrary, certainly the broad terms of the Act drew little definition from the older or the more recently made common law about restraint of trade.

Nonetheless, though the contemporary objectives were little defined, the enactment of the Sherman Act did have the effect of setting policy in important new directions. (1) Congress here formally acknowledged an ideal of free competition as an explicit value in our society, however vague its outline. The very declaration set up a rallying point for demands that would thenceforth exert continuous, if uneven, pressure on government. (2) Although Congress then little realized the force of what it was doing, it had formally acknowledged a corollary proposition, that the law had an affirmative obligation to maintain some measure of free competition. Common law probably had gone no further than to withhold judicial enforcement of illegal agreements; but now by statute government might bring criminal or civil actions against offenders and offending arrangements, and the statute provided treble damages to induce private suitors to use the right of action which it gave them. There is evidence that Congress thought the private suit would be the main positive instrument of enforcement; but, whatever it thought, it had in fact provided government a new opportunity to take the initiative and had thus inevitably added to the moral and political responsibility of government and its exposure to a new range of opinion pressure. (3) Moreover, the Sherman Act in fact increased the moral and political responsibility of the federal government to maintain the multi-state markets whose safety the central authorities had once to guarantee only against the parochialism of state action. In effect, the Sherman Act was a logical parallel to the new definition of federal responsibility expressed by the Interstate Commerce Act of 1887. (4) By its form—a direct, if vaguely defined command, enforceable in court—the Sherman Act put the shaping of policy into the hands of prosecutor and judge. This was so natural to the times as hardly to amount to a conscious choice among alternatives. Only three years before, Congress had created its first great regulatory administrative agency; the untested Interstate Commerce Commission had not had time to set a new pattern for economic control. Relying on the combination of prosecutor and judge, the Sherman Act thus in effect determined that lawyers, rather than politicians, economists, or administrators, would steer the development of anti-trust policy.[27]

There was little attention to anti-trust policy for about eight years after the Sherman Act. In 1895 the Supreme Court seemed to doom the Act to a narrow importance by its decision in the *Knight* (sugar trust) case. Manufacture was a matter of local concern, said the Court, and a combination of manufacturers could be deemed only of indirect effect on interstate commerce; the Sherman Act did not intend to apply to such combinations, and if it did so intend, the clear indication was that the Court would hold it unconstitutional. In 1898 Congress reacted to public concern over the first great merger movement by creating a fact-finding, policy-recommending Industrial Commission. In 1900–1901 Congress considered the Commission's report and some proposals to strengthen the Sherman Act, but could not work out much that would fit within the *Knight* decision. As a practical matter, only the Court could clear away this block. At this point President Theodore Roosevelt made his major contribution to the development of anti-trust policy, stimulating the Department of Justice to cast off the dead weight which the sugar trust decision had laid on prosecuting zeal. The Department brought suits which enabled the Court to reconsider its attitude, and in 1904 in the *Northern Securities* case a majority of the Court in substance repudiated the narrow implications of the *Knight* decision and reopened the door to vigorous federal action on behalf of the free market. From 1901 through his insurgent campaign of 1912, Roosevelt put anti-trust policy to the front of his program. Indirectly, he affected the course of policy by helping build popular acceptance of the anti-trust idea to a point approaching the solidity of a constitutional principle. But he never chose to exercise his skill in applying pressure to Congress to obtain any further legislative definition of the content of anti-trust policy. Probably his successful battle for more effective rate-making powers for the Interstate Commerce Commission exhausted his energy, or at any rate, in his shrewd estimation of popular limitations, exhausted the people's capacity for sustained interest. Moreover, Roosevelt characteristically wavered between his conviction that government must stay on top of the surge of social change and his worried concern lest there be too much disturbance of functioning institutions. He felt the lack of an assured theory of action with reference to this capital concentration problem, and this limited his reach.

Roosevelt did request one addition to federal anti-trust legislation, which Congress made by creating a Bureau of Corporations as part of a new Department of Commerce and Labor (1903). The Bureau was to find facts and publicize its findings for such regulatory effect as this publicity might have. With the President's support the Bureau launched into greater activity and probably had more effect on opinion than anticipated by conservative Congressmen who had thought the measure too innocuous to oppose. However, this measure was a preliminary to a program, and not the equivalent of one. Note of it may, therefore, appropriately conclude this sketch of nineteenth-century policy development concerning concentration of capital. The law had recognized that it should affirm and protect the social interest in the market. But the resources of imagination and will in the last generation of the century were not up to pushing the matter further.[28]

Apart from these problems of using law to shape an environment favorable to private individual and group liberty, there also began to emerge at the end of the century a new concern for the coherence and functional integrity of the community. Partly this was focused on sources of community strength, partly on community conditions deemed essential to a decent life for the individual.

On the whole, this attention to community integrity was not the security-conscious type of our colonial years. There was strain on community ties amid the tremendous social change of the century's last generation; federal troops moved against railroad strikers in 1877 and 1894; there was the Homestead strike riot of 1892, and the Haymarket bomb trial, the use of the injunction in labor disputes, the emotion surrounding the Presidential campaign of 1896. Except for the labor injunctions, however, most of this passed without wide or lasting expression in our law; there was nothing, for example, like the wave of state legislation against criminal syndicalism that came out of a disturbed middle-class opinion at the end of World War I. Considering the range and depth of change that was afoot from 1870 to 1910, the large immigration of people of village and peasant background, the juxtaposing of extremes of luxury, comfort, and hardness of life in the new metropolitan areas, the bitter years of debt and defeat in the grain states, one of the most striking aspects of the legal history of these years is how little evidence it affords of anything that can realistically be called conscious class conflict.

Interest group conflict in plenty marked statute books and judicial opinions. But the hard pressed positions and the angry tones among the major interests continued to be those of dispute within the family of middle-class values which had set the dominant policy tone of our society from our constitution-making generation on. The most pervasive evidence of this was steady, widespread political action based on faith that we could use law to mould a social environment favorable to private liberty. Trade unions accepted battle in the courts, even while they protested abuse of judicial power and sought corrective legislation; and unions invoked court protection of their internal order. Lobbyists for organized labor began to appear in state and federal legislative halls, seeking specific measures for specific grievances concerning safety at work, terms of wage payment, and importation of contract labor. In the presentation of such bills of particulars was implicit a practical acceptance of the evolving industrial order and of the idea of using law to help enforce for labor some participation in the decision making of industry. Big city bosses built their late-century power largely by the services which "the organization" rendered to socially isolated and disoriented immigrants; but awareness of social status distinction is not the same as consciousness of class division. The tactics of balancing religious or national-origin groups in a slate of candidates for metropolitan offices showed how conspicuously realistic contemporaries appraised prevailing popular values and convictions: so long as your kind of people showed a reasonable chance to make its way in the market, you would give your basic consent and faith to a community which made this possible. A good deal of flamboyant talk of "class" conflict colored the oratory of farm revolt in the nineties. But the morale of agrarian politics really rested on the continued Jeffersonian vision of a middle-class society of independent yeomen. "We desire a proper equality, equity and fairness," declared the National Grange: ". . . protection for the weak, restraint upon the strong; in short, justly distributed burdens and justly distributed power." Most revealing of the social conservatism of agrarian revolt was the position on the farmers' key issue of the railroads. The sustained demand was simply for regulation; Populist leaders called for government ownership, but the Democratic platform of 1896 stood by the demand for regulation which had been the mainstay of the Granger movement.[29]

Probably the pace of change after 1870 did as much as anything else to brake the development of a broad and lasting consciousness of class division. Events so hurried us from one society into another that we were living in a new order, with our old frames of reference, before we began fully to realize what had happened. With the pragmatism so ingrained in our working habits, we then began, piecemeal, to seek particular adjustments between our circumstances and our values—as in our trial-and-error development of a new body of public utility law. That we had begun our national history with a classic generation of constitution making provided a legal tradition which helped our efforts at pragmatic adjustment. We believed that we had in our constitutional framework an element of continuity amid all this change, providing means for peaceful accommodation. Of course, constitutionalism flowered partly in the extreme laissez faire doctrine which judges wrote into the due process clause as one reaction to the stresses of the end of the century. But the idea of constitutionally ordered power also expressed itself in a gathering flow of social legislation and in the mobilization of popular political power through legal means.

Manifest in end-of-century legislation was a rising concern not so much for the security of the society in any defensive sense, but rather for enforcing a more rational calculus in the total economy. For the first time we began to become cost conscious. Our statute books and our executive budgets reflected growing interest in promoting greater rationalization of social processes. Here were attitudes both consistent and inconsistent with the dominant public policy of the earlier part of the century. We continued to show faith that on an improved material base we could erect a more decent life for individuals; we continued deeply to believe that social good lay in the large release of individual and group energy expended upon production. We departed from our past as we groped toward a concept of social cost accounting. Much of our legislation amounted implicitly to a judgment that the decentralized, private cost accounting of the market did not suffice for efficient social living; that it did not strike a true balance of resources and input and output, but rather operated, willfully or not, to conceal subsidies and disguise burdens whose load must eventually fall on the society and to which the society, therefore, should openly assent.

Social cost accounting made a sizable beginning in the conservation of human resources before it was turned to deal with the other-than-human natural resources of the community. The thread of this story runs back into the 1840's. Evangelical religion then joined its emotional thrust to the rationalism we derived through Jefferson to produce the first substantial budgets for the care of the insane and of dependent and neglected children and old people, and the creation of some minimum standards in prisons. The first principal use of law here was, thus, through the power to allocate resources—directly by appropriation, indirectly by charters and tax exemptions granted private institutions. The contemporary temperance movement produced the first important use of legal regulation to protect human resources by prohibition or by restrictive licensing or special taxation of the liquor business.

To emphasize institutional care was inherently, at best, to emphasize remedy and restoration. The end of the century saw a major shift in policy direction toward prevention in programs involving both resources allocation and regulation. Growth in budgets for public health agencies and enactment of a widening range of sanitary legislation represented the law's assumption of a vast new responsibility for shaping the social environment. Most large cities created local boards of health between 1850 and 1875, but from the seventies it became the pattern also to set up state boards. Sanitary engineering went along with extended use of quarantine laws and regulation of the quality of water and milk supplies.

In addition the eighties brought legislation to conserve the community's labor supply and to mitigate the human costs of the machine. Statutes began to require the guarding of dangerous machines in factories, to limit or set special conditions upon employment of children and women, to set maximum hours of labor in certain jobs, to fix standards of fairness in the manner of wage payments. The law pertaining to the employer's liability to workers injured on the job became the focus of one of the longest, most stubborn legal battles of the last quarter of the century. The pull and haul was not only between employers and employees, but also between legislatures and judges whose strict construction of statutes changing common-law rules often destroyed the substance of legislative policy. Statutes limiting the employer's common-law defenses spread steadily through the industrial states, but the main effect of the courts' stubborn hostility was to underline the wastes and costs of litigious handling of the whole problem and to spur the adoption of the workmen's compensation system.

Slowest to develop was a third great field of public responsibility for the social environment—the protection of the ultimate consumer, now reduced to individual insignificance in the mass markets the law had helped to form. One set of problems had to do with sales of goods. Here common-law remedies by actions for damage negligently inflicted or for fraud and deceit or breach of warranty were expensive; the complaining party carried a difficult burden of proof against remote sellers or manufacturers, and the law was liberal in defenses offered the entrepreneur; the loss in the particular instance often was not big enough to warrant the trouble and cost of suit, though the aggregate of individual losses might represent a substantial total waste or oppression. From about 1881 the states began to legislate to protect consumers of food. After 1887 the United States Department of Agriculture became active primarily to protect farmers against fraudulent sellers of farm supplies. But not until the first, quite limited food and drugs and meat inspection laws of 1906 did the federal government move to protect ultimate consumers. In general, effective legal protection of consumers of goods is a twentieth-century story, centering as it does on the rise of the administrative process. It belongs in the history of nineteenth-century public policy principally for the emergence there of a new, recognized public responsibility.

The individual in our completely market-organized society depended as much on some essential services as he did on a supply of goods. Particularly he needed credit and insurance. The common law offered an oppressed debtor a defensive plea against enforcement of an usurious contract, and the courts would construe ambiguous terms of an insurance contract in favor of the insured, and might also stretch doctrines of waiver and estoppel to limit technical defenses set up by the insurance company. But to bring or defend a lawsuit was in itself a fearful venture to the average man, and the staying power of the longer purse was almost surely in the lender or the insurance company. Here again, effective answers lay in the twentieth-century history of administrative regulation and fostering of new sources of credit. But the nineteenth century did go a bit further than merely to acknowledge the problems. From the mid-eighties states began to limit the allowable terms of wage assignments and chattel mortgage loans, to require that the lender furnish the borrower a memorandum of their agreement and make reports of his business to a public office; Massachusetts pointed the way to what was to become the standard pattern of policy in the field when in 1898 it enacted a system for licensing lenders. From mid–nineteenth century states recognized a public responsibility for some surveillance of the financial soundness of insurance funds. More direct protection to the individual insured was afforded by legislative imposition of standard policy terms. In 1873 and 1886 Massachusetts and New York legislation provided the pressure which led the fire insurance industry to adopt a standard policy. Experience was not so successful with standard life policies, though these were tried after a recommendation of New York's Armstrong committee of 1906. However, legislation did materially improve the insured's position by specifically requiring insertion of key protective clauses and specifically banning insertion of types of defensive language which had worked injustice. However limited its range, statutory treatment of both the small loans and the insurance problems thus effectively used the standardization which legislation can provide to limit the range and incidence of controversy.[30]

There had been moral idealism and religiously fired concern for human dignity to support the beginnings of policy for the conservation of human resources. For most of the nineteenth century there were no comparable attitudes to stimulate concern about waste and inefficiency in the use of our other natural endowment. Indeed, the prevailing attitude ran wholly to the opposite result. Looking upon our wealth, we found it obviously "inexhaustible"—the adjective recurs ritually in public and private documents—and drew the conclusion that we should press our present ambitions by whatever seemed the quickest route. Rapid settlement and productive expansion were unquestionable values. Wisconsin's Governor Harvey struck the common note in exhorting the 1862 legislature:

A comprehensive State policy must take in every judicious measure inviting capital and labor to the development of our resources. The census of 1860 shows 3,746,036 acres of the area of Wisconsin to be improved, while 4,153,134 acres are unimproved. Our State is rich, far beyond all she now enjoys, in capabilities of production—in forests of timber—in unappropriated water power, and in latent mineral wealth. These vast resources need but the touch of labor and capital for the realization of the wildest dreams of prosperity for our State.[31]

Whether the record was of premature depletion of energy sources (as in fruitless burning off of natural gas or improper drilling for oil), the pollution of water supply and destruction of fish life (through dumping of mineral or industrial cast-offs), the exhaustion of game (by reckless commercial hunting of pigeons, geese, or buffalo, for example), or soil erosion or air pollution, the story of nineteenth-century public policy ran the same course. First we wasted natural resources because we could not see their use or because they were in the way of some immediate goal. Next our expanding markets would suddenly produce a rush and a scale of demand which encouraged headlong, unplanned profit taking. At some point, usually no earlier than in the eighties, would begin to develop the consciousness that exhaustion or scarcity was not impossible, even in the midst of our opportunities. In most areas, again, nineteenth-century policy wound up at best by acknowledging the existence of a problem and a responsibility.

Benchmarks of change in Wisconsin forest policy demonstrate this typical progression. In 1867 a legislative committee recommended creation of a temporary commission to consider public policy concerning the state's forest resources. Looking back, the committee identified the first stage in the state's timber history, where trees were simply a hindrance to the agricultural settler:

It is true there are cases where it has been necessary to clear off the forests and plow up the grubs, that the land may be cultivated for food; but it is well known that thousands of acres of the best timber of Wisconsin has been cut down and burned in the log heaps, or sent to the markets of the towns at prices which have only paid cost of cutting and transportation. Lands have thus been stripped of timber which are now little better than wastes, the timber on which, had it been allowed to remain, would, by its increased value, have paid all taxes and interest on its first cost, leaving a large surplus to its owner. . . .

Many of our inhabitants have come from parts where trees and woods were considered nuisances, to be removed. Such have never asked themselves what would be the consequences to themselves and their posterity, by this systematic destruction of the natural groves of the state. Others, who at first selected for a building spot for their homes a site sheltered by trees, have found themselves, a few years after, exposed to the full blasts of the winds, because in a thoughtless moment, they cut a field out of their protector.

The committee observed that the sudden opening of an insatiable market for timber in the grain states to the west had already plunged Wisconsin into the second stage of heedless exploitation of its great northern pine forest:

The northern woods at present afford timber for building purposes. But those woods are fast passing from us—faster than those who have given but little thought to the subject believe. Hundreds, if not thousands, of millions of feet of our best pines are annually cut down and run out of the state, to supply the prairies of our neighbors.[32]

The legislature passed the recommended bill, instructing the commission to inquire

whether, owing to the want of information in individuals and the shortness of their lives, it is the duty of the state to interfere [interpose] its authority to prevent an undue destruction of forest trees where they now exist, and to encourage their cultivation where they are deficient.

The error in the verb, which the printer of the session laws undertook to correct by his bracketed insertion, more accurately expressed the temper of 1867 than the unusually farsighted bill or committee report. The commission reported in strong terms on the "disastrous effects of the destruction of forest trees now going on so rapidly in the state of Wisconsin," but the only consequence was the enactment in 1868 of a mild tax exemption to encourage farmers to plant protective tree belts. Aside from some efforts to provide more efficient organization against forest fires, the state did nothing more about timber conservation until an

1897 statute provided for a commission to plan a system of state forest reserves and to study the best future use of forest resources. Characteristically, action following the new commission's studies waited upon the twentieth century.[33]

Deep in the background of late nineteenth-century efforts at least to define felt problems and to acknowledge new-sensed responsibilities were changes in attitudes and approach which would grow into dominant characteristics of our twentieth-century legal history.

Some of the values and attitudes which supplied the dynamics of our emerging concern with the balance of power and the conservation of human and natural resources were obvious enough, if striking in their juxtaposition. Both the religious and the rationalist elements in our tradition contributed insistent regard for the dignity of the individual life and humanitarian treatment of individuals in trouble. Our position in the main stream of middle-class growth meant that we valued nothing more highly than the mobility that went with political and social equality and the economic efficiency needed to realize our faith that production could provide a material base for the fulfillment of men's spirit.

But a new factor affected our working philosophy and the consequent demands which substantial opinion made upon law in the last quarter of the century. This was a realignment of our notions of man's place in the world and of the relative significance of the various challenges which circumstances opposed to his freedom. The speed with which capital concentration changed the distribution of power shocked us into an attention to the political management of social environment such as we had not given since 1800. The primary reflection of this was in the pull and haul of interest groups. But these efforts to enlist men's allegiances brought an unexpected consequence. They bred a sharper awareness of the patterns of interest in our evolving social structure; this new sense of pattern taught a fresh appreciation of social interdependence not only to practical politicians and lawmakers but also to a growing body of "independent" voter opinion. Symptomatic was the way in which the firsthand explorations of Assemblyman Theodore Roosevelt in 1882 into the conditions of home cigar manufacture in lower East Side tenements produced the conviction with which Governor Theodore Roosevelt drove through the New York legislature in 1899 his program of labor legislation. Consciousness of the challenge of social environment thus fostered concern not only for the balance of power but also for the functional soundness of society.[34]

Our attitude toward the challenge of physical environment changed also. At first we had seen this challenge rather simply, as a matching of man-made force against natural inertia, of the settler's muscle against the trees and rocks he must clear away to make tillable land. But after 1850 dramatic changes in science and technology taught people to estimate the challenge of physical environment as one which lay more in our ignorance than in nature's opposition. Popular notions of what we could do to enlarge men's options and reduce burdens on life generated popular demands that we do it. Pressure groups enlisted in some of these causes, but knowledge spread abroad could itself become a source of political dynamics; it was no Anti-Germ League, but rather a massive public opinion informed of discoveries in bacteriology which supported extension of sanitation laws.[35]

Another yet more subtle change marked our perception of reality in relation to men's liberties. Much sentimentality and irrelevant moralizing went into mid-century movements for better organized care of those who fell below the social margin—the insane, the delinquent, the drunkard. But reports of public welfare institutions toward the end of the century began to recognize that people might be in trouble because they were trapped within their own limitations of emotion and ignorance. In this aspect budgets for public institutions responded to a third kind of environmental limit on men's freedom, that constituted by the configuration of personality. The public school system expressed primarily the values we put on political and social mobility. But in a measure it, too, began to reflect the sense of this scarcely defined challenge of men's inner environment. Once we had outlined a policy of sanitary controls of the general environment, we began to control disease by changing personal ways of life. This meant control by the spread of knowledge, largely through public school hygiene and physical education programs, and the work of public clinics and tax exempt private health associations. Thus law allocated community resources to enlarge liberty by helping individuals to restructure the habits and beliefs which make of personality a kind of limiting environment. The twentieth century added emphasis on mental hygiene to make the direction of this policy still clearer.[36]

Changes in methods of analyzing issues and implementing policy developed toward the end of the nineteenth century—changes which, like the altered definitions of environmental challenge, would broaden into major trends of twentieth-century law.

A good deal of melodrama is inherent in a politics which must interest a wide public; there must be heroes and villains and plenty of action or the appearance of action. But our public policy tended to grow from

1800 to 1890 in a more highly charged atmosphere than this minimum requirement of political practice called for. The primacy of the release-of-energy principle, with its implicit stress on the free and responsible wills of individuals, encouraged us to draw all public issues in moral terms, of good men versus bad men. The immediacy of the physical and social challenge of the unopened continent prodded us to value vigorous action for its own sake. Both the moralistic and activist bias were at a high point, for example, in the drama of Andrew Jackson against Nicholas Biddle; and the limitations of this bias were amply displayed in the result, which completely disregarded the functional requirements of our market society for a centralized credit system under public regulation. The same unduly simplified approach, borne on a tide of emotion and demands for action, marked Granger efforts to regulate railroad rates by statutory fiat. The creation of a national banking organization and the beginnings of administrative regulation of the railroads expressed a turn toward a more matter-of-fact use of law to shape the environment. It was a direction of events symbolized by Theodore Roosevelt's anti-trust policy, with its combination of moral jeremiads and a fact-collecting, fact-analyzing Bureau of Corporations.

The trend toward a more matter-of-fact development of public policy involved three closely related changes in techniques of social control. The first was a tendency to think more in terms of engineering-minded arrangements or rearrangements of social forces, and less in terms of moral exhortation. Mid-century policy had used law to help mobilize scattered capital; now we used law to mobilize scattered political force, to gather in otherwise diffuse and ill-defined demands and wants and, by channelling them, to build up effective pressure.

In part we did this by direct use of public funds. We expanded national and state executive budgets, enlarging familiar offices to handle new functions and creating new administrative agencies of mixed legislative, executive, and judicial powers. The functional impact of much of this was to set up publicly supported "lobbies" to represent the otherwise dispersed power of shippers, consumers of essential services, and buyers of goods, as they confronted integrated and disciplined utilities and sellers in an impersonal market.

We had delegated to private hands power to raise capital by eminent domain and tolls; so now we delegated to private hands enlarged capacities to mobilize political force, increasing the number of people with some effective voice in policy making. Extension of the suffrage to Negroes and to women followed a policy firmly set since Jacksonian days. Less familiar were devices which, in fashion somewhat like eminent domain, helped those not within the inner circles of private might to appropriate some portion of private power preserves to public use. Thus through registration of lobbyists and publicity of their efforts the elder LaFollette sought to provide more leverage for the less organized against the more regimented interests within the community. At the turn of the century the movement to reorganize procedures for political expression of power—through the direct primary, the short ballot, the initiative, referendum, and recall—had the same character. Earlier in the century by grants of discretionary powers to fix tolls we had delegated to utilities entrepreneurs a considerable power to draft capital contributions to their enterprises. The justification, of course, was that while this might serve private interest, it also fulfilled public needs. Now by the doctrine that legislation should enjoy the benefit of a "presumption of constitutionality," courts in effect conceded the propriety of delegating to private pressure groups substantial discretion in initiating and defining public policy by statute. As a principle important to the practical operation of the separation of powers, the Supreme Court had early recognized that judges owed deference to legislative determinations and should not substitute their weighting of equities for that struck by the legislators. This doctrine took on fresh, added meaning when politics moved into an era of more organized group influence on legislation. Of course, the presumption of constitutionality collided head-on with the laissez faire bias which ran strongly through the late-century judicial reaction to the broadening flow of social legislation. Nonetheless, key decisions affirmed the presumption, and though many cases implicitly denied it force, it remained the acknowledged central principle of judicial review.[87]

A second change in our approach to social control involved closer attention to the nature and incidence of the costs of policy. This attitude developed slowly, but by the turn of the century several basic propositions in social cost accounting were already implicit in our legal development.

First, policy making began to acknowledge the existence of social costs. This was elementary, but our continental abundance had taught us for 250 years to be careless of reckonings. In particular we had to learn that inertia or default of policy could produce costs, just as much as could some positive decision. To do nothing when factories dumped destructive refuse into streams was in effect to decide that more rapid industrialization was worth the community costs of losing fish and erecting facilities to purify drinking water. Much end-of-century economic regulation tacitly acknowledged that we had been making such cost decisions without recognizing the fact.

Second, we had to decide sometime how far we would live on capital rather than on income. Again, inaction might be in effect decision. From 1860 to 1900 Wisconsin allowed the insistent lumber demand of the treeless prairie states to set the heedless pace at which its great forest was stripped. This undoubtedly hastened the growth of midwest agriculture. But it was a growth which we paid for out of social capital, not income, insofar as we destroyed the forest instead of cropping it. The belated provision in 1897 for a study of state forestry policy acknowledged that the situation involved a responsibility which law could not shirk indefinitely.

Third, efficiency and equity required that public subsidies to private persons be openly assessed, and not accomplished by inattention or concealment. For want of adequately enforced bans on railroad rebates the market situation from the seventies on worked a covert capital subsidy to powerful shippers and thereby accelerated the unbalanced concentration of private power. Toleration of child labor subsidized industries by allowing them to enjoy a cheaper wage bill; the community in the long run paid the difference, in disease and in educational deficiencies which reacted on the social stock of political and economic skills.

Finally, we had to learn that the incidence of cost was socially as important as the fact that cost existed. In the mid-century enthusiasm for the release-of-energy principle, we favored action. A man did not act at his peril; an injured person must show particular reason why law should shift from his shoulders part of his loss, to be borne by the one who caused injury. But machinery began enormously to multiply the hazards of work and life; at the same time production and distribution came to be conducted predominantly by organized groups, the expansion of markets made possible low unit overhead costs, and we acquired much more experience in the business of insurance. Gradually we concluded that it was not only unfair but inefficient to make injured individuals bear losses causally related to our new scale of economic operations when these losses might readily and painlessly be spread among those who benefited by the operations. Law expressed this reassessment of the situation in employers' liability legislation, in expanded statutory responsibility of the makers of goods, and in stricter judge-made law on the liability of principals for the wrongdoing of their agents.[38]

The third major trend after 1870 in the development of techniques of forming and implementing policy was the great increase in reliance on government fact collecting and analysis. From the start of our national life, we made important use of government to advance knowledge for immediately practical objects in shaping our environment. Through provision for the census the Constitution itself made social science research a federal obligation; the Lewis and Clark expedition (1804) and the creation of the coastal survey (1807) attest how early executive and legislative practice followed the same policy; state census or statistics gathering projects and geological surveys began before 1850. But after 1860, in response to closer social interdependence, we groped toward continuous, management functions of law which inevitably gave data collection and analysis such central importance as they had never before enjoyed. If the impetus toward this end was largely in the needs of administration, it lay also in practical politics. What people knew, or at least believed, could be a powerful element in generating demands on government; and as government administration developed facilities for fact gathering and analysis, this development, partly deliberately and partly by simple institutional drive, became a significant source of policy movement.

In 1862 the federal government took a decisive step in this new factual emphasis with the creation of the Department of Agriculture. Within its first twenty years the Department made basic research a principal instrument of its influence. Significant for the institutional drive toward fact collection and analysis as sources of policy was the establishment of the Interstate Commerce Commission in 1887. Charles Francis Adams made investigation and publicity the central functions of the Board of Railroad Commissioners which Massachusetts set up in 1869. Experience proved that this was an inadequate role for such a regulatory body; but the effort authoritatively recognized that the increase and dissemination of knowledge were indispensable to the shaping role of law in the kind of a society we had developed. Felix Frankfurter appraises Florence Kelley's work as the first chief factory inspector of Illinois in terms which sum up the mingled political and administrative significance of the fact-handling job of government:

There are two kinds of reformers whose chief concern has been that earning a living shall not contradict living a life. One type is apt to see evil men behind evils and seeks to rout evil by moral fervor. Florence Kelley belonged to the other, the cooler and more calculating type. Not that she was without passion. But passion was the driving force of her mind, not its substitute. She early realized that damning facts are more powerful in the long run than flaming rhetoric, and that understanding is a more dependable, because more permanent ally than the indignation of the moment. . . . She went about winning cohorts, men and women whose consciences she could ignite, and whose minds she could educate to serve as constructive guides to their consciences. She realized that a few people who cared, and who knew why they cared, would serve as infectious forces in influencing their environment. . . . From the beginning of her work as a chief inspector of factories for Illinois, she realized the importance of effective administration and all that it implies—a system of alert oversight, a permanent, trained, non-political inspectorate, reliable statistics, illuminating reports as the basis of continuous public education. . . .[39]

After seventy-five years of living from day to day amid the surge of an opening continent, we did not suddenly after 1870 become a nation of social philosophers. Most significant lines of policy direction in the last quarter of the nineteenth century were only implicit in our legal history. But our conduct did declare some working principles in the statutes we passed, the administration we developed, the lawsuits we fought. These working principles constituted an inheritance of experience and choice which, however imperfect, largely set the framework within which domestic policy grew through the first half of the twentieth century. We continued to believe in an institutional pattern which allowed the large release of energy by private individuals and groups. However, to an increasing degree it was groups rather than individuals which exercised this liberty. We had much yet to learn about how to fulfill individual freedom in a group-organized society. We continued also to hold and indeed to strengthen the confidence that we could by law measurably shape environment to our ends. The issue here was over relative emphasis on competing objectives. In the unsettlement of two World Wars and the rise of the Russian challenge, we put a higher premium on community security than we had since our colonial years. Given our traditionally unphilosophic and unhistoric habit of mind, there was danger that we would not appreciate how much our past security had resided, first, in the acceptance of difference that was involved in the release-of-energy principle and, second, in the positively creative thrust of the policy of controlling environment to enlarge men's practical freedom. We had not built what we had in a defensive frame of mind; but it was not clear how far broad opinion recognized the implications of this. Moreover, to pursue effectively the policy of enlarging men's options required that we learn better how to deal with increasingly powerful, limited-objective pressure groups and how to generate support for critically important areas of environment control—such as the encouragement of basic research—toward which existing pressure groups were indifferent, if not hostile. Such challenges insistently demanded of us more deliberate and self-conscious policy making than had characterized the nineteenth-century record.

NOTES

1. Lothrop's account of the Pike Creek history, including a copy of the constitution of the Pike River Claimants Union, is contained in 8th Wis. Legis. (1856), J. Ass., App. Vol. 2, pp. 472–475; cf. id., pp. 475–479 (Constitution of the Milwaukee Union). See also Frank, *Early History of Kenosha,* 9th Wis. Legis. (1857), J. Ass., App. Vol. 2, pp. 370–394, at 378, 386–387; Mygatt, *Some Account of the First Settlement of Kenosha, id.,* pp. 395–420, at 409. On the claims associations generally, see Hibbard, *A History of the Public Land Policies* (New York, 1939), pp. 198–208; Schafer, *Four Wisconsin Counties* (Madison, 1927), pp. 69–80.

2. The release-of-energy faith demonstrated in our law expressed one aspect of a social value scale which measured men by their accomplishment in striving toward self-appointed material goals, rather than by their status. See Horney, *The Neurotic Personality of Our Time* (New York, 1937), pp. 288–289; Mead, *And Keep Your Powder Dry* (New York, 1942), pp. 67–69, 91, 93, 113, 202; Williams, *American Society* (New York, 1951), pp. 390–394.

3. *Cf.* Hamilton, Report on the Subject of Manufactures, 1 Reports of the Secretary of the Treasury 78, 85 (Washington, 1837); 1 H. C. Carey, *Principles of Political Economy* 337–342 (Philadelphia, 1837–1840); Bancroft, *The Office of the People in Art, Government and Religion,* in *Literary and Historical Miscellanies* (New York, 1855), p. 408; 2 Tocqueville, *Democracy in America* 41–47 (Bradley, ed. New York, 1945); George, *Progress and Poverty* (50th anniversary ed. New York, 1932), pp. 3–4, 255–260.

4. Locke, *Essay on Civil Government* (1690), Ch. XI; 12 & 13 William III, c. 3 (1700), 10 Statutes at Large 360 (1764); *The Federalist* (Lodge, ed. New York, 1888), No. 78 (Hamilton), pp. 484, 487–489; *cf.* Webster, *The Basis of the Senate,* in 3 *Works* 8, 14, 16 (8th ed. 6 vols. Boston, 1854). See, generally, 6 Holdsworth, *A History of English Law* 82–83, 103, 150, 251, 288, 359 (Boston, 1927); Larkin, *Property in the Eighteenth Century* (Dublin, 1930), pp. 112–124, 149–151, 155–156, 164, 172; Knappen, *Constitutional and Legal History of England* (New York, 1942), p. 377; Miller, J., in *Loan Association* v. *Topeka,* 20 Wall. 655, 662–664 (U.S. 1874).

5. *Cf.* Sumner, *The Challenge of Facts* in *The Challenge of Facts and Other Essays* (Keller, ed. New Haven, 1914), p. 17.

6. Compare: "The commercial law should be thought of as a coherent sys-

tem whereby economic cooperation is sought to be reconciled with an individualistic philosophy of life." Gardner, *An Inquiry into the Principles of the Law of Contracts,* 46 Harv. L. Rev. 1, 42 (1932); on the delegation of the law's power implicit in contract, see *id.,* pp. 5, 7, 20, 22, 23; and Fuller, *Consideration and Form,* 41 Col. L. Rev. 799, 806, 808–810 (1941).

7. 6 Corbin, *On Contracts* 459 (St. Paul, 1951).

8. See Fuller, *op. cit. supra* note 6; Kessler, *Corbin on Contracts: Formation of Contracts,* 61 Yale L.J. 1092, 1101 (1952); on the mysteries of consideration, and contrary currents in its development, see 1 Corbin, *op. cit. supra* note 7, at 346; Pound, *Individual Interests of Substance—Promised Advantages,* 69 Harv. L. Rev. 1, 29–32 (1945).

9. *Miller v. Larson,* 19 Wis. 463, 466 (1865), and *Morse v. Ryan,* 26 Wis. 356, 362 (1870); see, also, *Fay v. Oatley,* 6 Wis. 42, 54–55 (1865); *Gilmore v. Roberts,* 79 Wis. 450, 453, 48 N.W. 522, 523 (1891).

10. *Barrows v. Jackson,* 346 U.S. 249, 253–254 (1953); see *Shelley v. Kraemer,* 334 U.S. 1, 17–18, 22 (1948).

11. See Kessler, *op. cit. supra* note 8, at 1097; Rheinstein, ed., *Max Weber on Law in Economy and Society* (Cambridge, 1954), pp. 39–40, 100, 101, 105.

12. Sir George Jessel, M.R., in *Printing and Numerical Registering Co. v. Sampson,* (1875) L.R. 19 Eq. 462, 465; *cf. Diamond Match Co. v. Roeber,* 106 N.Y. 473, 13 N.E. 419 (1887); *Williams v. Phelps,* 16 Wis. 80, 86 (1862); *Chippewa Valley & Superior Railway Co. v. Chicago, St. Paul, Minneapolis & Omaha Railway Co.,* 75 Wis. 224, 244, 44 N.W. 17, 22 (1889); *Trump v. Shoudy,* 166 Wis. 353, 359, 164 N.W. 454, 456 (1917); *W. M. Bell Co. v. Emberson,* 182 Wis. 433, 446–447, 196 N.W. 861, 866 (1924). See Peppin, *Price-Fixing Agreements under the Sherman Anti-Trust Law,* 28 Calif. L. Rev. 297, 350 (1940); Pound, *op. cit. infra* note 18, at 268. On the courts' unwillingness to weigh the adequacy of consideration, see 1 Corbin, *op. cit. supra* note 7, at 392.

13. 2 Tocqueville, *op. cit. supra* note 3, at 157.

14. See 1 Stimson, *American Statute Law* (Boston, 1886), pp. 97–99, 146; Osborne, *Mortgages* (St. Paul, 1951), pp. 31–41.

15. Debates and Proceedings in the New York State Convention for the Revision of the Constitution (Albany, 1846), p. 805 (remarks of Mr. Harris); see Christman, *Tin Horns and Calico* (New York, 1945), pp. 2–14, 258–260. *Cf.* Brown, *The Making of the Wisconsin Constitution,* 1949 Wis. L. Rev. 548, 684, n. 98; Van Alstyne, *Land Transfer and Recording in Wisconsin* (Unpublished S.J.D. Thesis, on deposit in the Law Library, University of Wisconsin); Report, Committee on Incorporations, 1st Wis. Legis., J. Sen., July 21, 1848, p. 219, at 220, and Report of Select Committee on Bill No. 68, *id.,* Aug. 15, 1848, p. 399; Report, Committee on Public Lands, 2d Wis. Legis., J. Sen., Jan. 26, 1849, p. 92, at 93, 98; Opinion of the Attorney General on a land ownership limitation bill, 4th Wis. Legis., J. Ass., Feb. 19, 1851, pp. 374–375.

16. See Isaacs, *The Standardization of Contracts,* 27 Yale L.J. 34, 35–36 (1917); Kessler, *op. cit. supra* note 8, at 1096; Llewellyn, *On the Complexity of Consideration: A Foreword,* 41 Col. L. Rev. 777, 782 (1941) (contract is "a body of doctrine about *day to day transactions* which originated in Elizabeth's

time, which was built heavily in a 19th Century that had only begun to foreshadow modern conditions. . . ."), and his *On the Good, the True, the Beautiful in Law,* 9 U. Chi. L. Rev. 224, 235, 237–238 (1942); Radin, *Contract Obligation and the Human Will,* 43 Col. L. Rev. 575, 576–577 (1943).

17. Legal bibliography furnishes a ready measure of the tide of interest and invention in all the forms of contract. Blackstone put into about 45 pages all that he found necessary to say about business contracts. I Blackstone, *Commentaries on the Laws of England* 246–247 (4 vols. Oxford, 1769); 2 *id.* 296–297, 300–305, 397–398, 442–471; 3 *id.* 154–158, 161–164, 434–435. By the end of the nineteenth century's first quarter, Kent was impelled to give contract and its related commercial subjects space amounting to about one out of his four volumes. 2 Kent, *Commentaries on American Law* (4 vols. New York, 1826–1830) 321–331 (insolvency), 363–437 (sales of goods), 437–477 (bailments), 477–509 (principal and agent), 509–528 (history of maritime law); 3 *id.* 1–45 (partnership), 43–92 (negotiable paper), 93–306 (law of the sea, affreightment, insurance, maritime loans). The work of the two standard text writers of the middle of the century dramatically reflects the expansion of contract to a dominant position in that period of legal development. Story published his *Bailments* (1832—to run into nine editions), *Conflict of Laws* (1834, eight editions), *Equity Jurisprudence* (1836, 13 American editions), *Equity Pleadings* (1838, 10 editions), *Agency* (1839, nine editions), *Partnership* (1841, seven editions), *Bills of Exchange* (1843, four editions), and *Promissory Notes* (1845, seven editions). Parsons published *The Law of Contracts* (2 vols. 1853–1855), *The Elements of Mercantile Law* (1856, 1862), *The Laws of Business* (1857), *A Treatise on Maritime Law* (2 vols. 1859), *A Treatise on the Law of Promissory Notes and Bills of Exchange* (2 vols. 1836, 1876), *A Treatise on the Law of Partnership* (1867), *A Treatise on the Law of Marine Insurance and General Average* (2 vols. 1868), and *A Treatise on the Law of Shipping* (2 vols. 1869). See Pound, *The Formative Era in American Law* (New York, 1938), and the useful discussion of the growth of legal protection of the security of transactions in an impersonal market, in Isaacs, *Business Postulates and the Law,* 41 Harv. L. Rev. 1014 (1928).

Though much legislation was declaratory of court-made doctrine, the nineteenth-century statute books reflect the importance of the growth of contract in the law of the century. See 1 Stimson, *op. cit. supra* note 14, at 282–294 (mechanics liens), 447–496 (contracts), 497–524 (bailments), 504–507, 530–541 (security interests in personalty), 541–560 (sales), 570–571 (bottomry and respondentia bonds), 571–593 (negotiable instruments), 593–601 (finance), 561–568 (liens, generally); Stimson, *Popular Law-Making* (New York, 1911), pp. 148–151, 153, 154. On liens and creditor-debtor relations generally, see Farnam, *Chapters in the History of Social Legislation in the United States to 1860* (Day, ed. Washington, 1938), pp. 152–156; *cf.* Wis. Rev. Stats., 1878, secs. 3329–3342 (liens on logs and lumber for labor, supplies, and services).

18. See Fuller, *op. cit. supra* note 6, at 808, 811; Isaacs, *op. cit. supra* note 16, at 35, 38, 46; Kessler, *op. cit. supra* note 8, at 1100, 1101, and his *Contracts of Adhesion—Some Thoughts about Freedom of Contract,* 43 Col. L. Rev. 629, 630 (1943); Patterson, *Corbin on Contracts: Construction and Legal*

Operation of Contracts—Conditions of Legal Duty, 61 Yale L.J. 1113, 1114 (1952); Pound, *Introduction to the Philosophy of Law* (New Haven, 1922), pp. 230, 268–269, and *op. cit. supra* note 8, at 29; Radin, *op. cit. supra* note 16, at 575, 577.

19. Compare the difference in approach in the Veto Message of Gov. Farwell, 6th Wis. Legis., J. Sen., June 6, 1853, pp. 815–817 (charter of Chippewa River Improvement & Navigation Co.); in the 19 vetoes filed by Gov. Randall, 11th Wis. Legis., J. Ass., March 4–May 17, pp. 826–830, 857, 871, 1013–1016, 1063, 1089, 1318, 1762, 2102; and that of Gov. Harvey, 15th Wis. Legis., J. Sen., March 8, 1862, p. 474 (Eau Claire River Log Driving Co.). See, generally, Henderson, *The Position of Foreign Corporations in American Constitutional Law* (Cambridge, 1918), Ch. I, and pp. 19–21, 66–69; 1 Kirkland, *Men, Cities and Transportation* 116–119, 127, 132–134, 141, 326–328 (Cambridge, 1948); *Gloucester Ferry Co.* v. *Pennsylvania,* 114 U.S. 196, 204–205 (1885).

20. Dodd, *American Business Corporations Until 1860* (Cambridge, 1954), and Evans, *Business Incorporations in the United States, 1800–1943* (New York, 1948), are basic. Legal history is much indebted also to the stimulating studies sponsored by the Committee on Research in Economic History, of the Social Science Research Council, notably, Handlin and Handlin, *Commonwealth: Massachusetts, 1774–1861* (New York, 1947), Hartz, *Economic Policy and Democratic Thought: Pennsylvania, 1776–1860* (Cambridge, 1948), and Kirkland, *op. cit. supra* note 19; see Cadman, *The Corporation in New Jersey* (Cambridge, 1949); Heath, *Constructive Liberalism: The Role of the State in Economic Development in Georgia to 1860* (Cambridge, 1954); Primm, *Economic Policy in the Development of a Western State: Missouri, 1820–1860* (Cambridge, 1954). See, also, Kuehnl, *The Wisconsin Business Corporation, 1800–1875* (Unpublished S.J.D. Thesis, on deposit in the Law Library, University of Wisconsin). On the late nineteenth-century invention, or inventive remodeling, of financial procedures, see Stetson, and others, *Some Legal Phases of Corporate Financing, Reorganization and Regulation* (New York, 1930); Stimson, *Popular Law-Making* (New York, 1911), p. 120; Winkelman, *John G. Johnson* (Philadelphia, 1942), p. 238.

21. 2 Tocqueville, *op. cit. supra* note 3, at 156–157.

22. Jackson, J., for the Court, in *Morisette* v. *United States,* 342 U.S. 246, 250, 251–252, and authorities cited in notes 4–9 thereof (1952). The research has not been done which would tell us whether the criminal law as administered by the police and the trial courts in fact conformed to the emphasis which appellate courts and text writers put on intention. But the appellate opinions and the texts at least evidence what were the formally expressed values of the times.

23. *Commonwealth* v. *Carlisle,* Bright. 36, 38–39 (Pa. 1821). I am indebted for the citation to Harno, *Intent in Criminal Conspiracy,* 89 U. Pa. L. Rev. 624 (1941), an essay which should be examined on the general theme here discussed; see, also, his *Some Significant Developments in Criminal Law and Procedure in the Last Century,* 42 J. Crim. Law, Criminology and Police Science 427, 429–432 (1951). *Cf.* Livingston Hall, *The Substantive Law of Crimes—1887–1936,* 50 Harv. L. Rev. 616, 622–634, 641–647 (1937); Hurst, *Treason in the United States,* 58 Harv. L. Rev. 806, 814–827 (1945). Also rele-

vant to my theme is the nineteenth-century curbing of earlier precedents which appeared to make trade-unions criminal conspiracies without regard to objectives or methods. See Gregory, *Labor and the Law* (rev. ed. New York, 1946), Ch. I, and Nelles, *Commonwealth* v. *Hunt*, 32 Col. L. Rev. 1128, 1148, 1151, 1163–1166 (1932). See, generally, Pound, *Criminal Justice in America* (New York, 1930), pp. 11–26, 31–35, 52, 57–58, 105–106, 112, 116, 131–133, 135–138.

24. *Brown* v. *Kendall*, 60 Mass. 292 (1850); *cf. Richards* v. *Sperry*, 2 Wis. 216 (1853). The high point of this value judgment was its erection by the New York Court of Appeals into a constitutional principle, in *Ives* v. *South Buffalo R. Co.*, 201 N.Y. 271, 94 N.E. 431 (1911). *New York Central R.R. Co.* v. *White*, 243 U.S. 188 (1917), however, made plain that, so far as the Fourteenth Amendment was concerned, it lay within reasonable legislative discretion to decide when and how far the fault basis of liability suited social needs. Compare Friedmann, *Social Insurance and the Principles of Tort Liability*, 63 Harv. L. Rev. 241, 261–265 (1949).

25. *Guinard* v. *Knapp-Stout & Co., Company*, 95 Wis. 482, 487, 70 N.W. 671, 672 (1897); compare the later re-evaluation in legislation and decisions, reflected in *West* v. *Bayfield Mill Co.*, 144 Wis. 106, 128 N.W. 992 (1910), and *Krueck* v. *Phoenix Chair Co.*, 157 Wis. 266, 147 N.W. 41 (1914). See Commons, *Myself* (New York, 1934), pp. 141–143, 153–160; Ehrenzweig, *Negligence Without Fault* (Berkeley and Los Angeles, 1951), p. 16.

26. *Wright* v. *E. E. Bolles Wooden Ware Co.*, 50 Wis. 167, 170–171, 6 N.W. 508, 510 (1880).

27. *Hadley* v. *Baxendale*, 9 Exch. 341 (1854); *Shepard* v. *Milwaukee Gas Light Co.*, 15 Wis. 318, 328 (1862); see 5 Corbin, *op. cit. supra* note 7, at 61–64, and 6 *id.* at 476, 478; Gardner, *op. cit. supra* note 6, at 29; Patterson, *The Apportionment of Business Risks Through Legal Devices*, 24 Col. L. Rev. 335, 342 (1924). *Cf.* Kapp, *The Social Costs of Private Enterprise* (Cambridge, 1950), pp. 230–231. Of analogous import is the rule that the promisee may recover only for unavoidable losses consequent upon the promisor's breach. Gardner, *loc. cit. supra*, at 31; *Clark* v. *Marsiglia*, 1 Denio 317 (N.Y. 1845); *Chapman* v. *Ingram*, 30 Wis. 290 (1872).

28. See Llewellyn, *On the Good, the True, the Beautiful in Law*, 9 U. Chi. L. Rev. at 240–241 (1942); Nelles, *op. cit. supra* note 23, at 1128, 1152 (1932); Pound, *op. cit. supra* note 18, at 166–168, 175. *Cf.* 46th Wis. Legis., J. Sen., Feb. 18, 1903, pp. 342–343.

29. Jerome Hall, *Theft, Law and Society* (2d ed. Indianapolis, 1935), Ch. II; Livingston Hall, *loc. cit. supra* note 23, at 617.

30. Evans, J., in *Murray* v. *South Carolina Railroad Co.*, 1 McM. 385, 399 (So. C. 1841); see *Milwaukee & Mississippi R.R. Co.* v. *Finney*, 10 Wis. 388, 394 (1860). *Cf.* Story, *Commentaries on the Law of Agency* (Boston, 1839), p. 465; Wigmore, *Responsibility for Tortious Acts*, 7 Harv. L. Rev. 383, 392–394, 398 (1894); Isaacs, *Fault and Liability*, 31 *id.* 954, 967 (1918); Douglas, *Vicarious Liability and Administration of Risk*, 38 Yale L.J. 584 (1929); James, *Accident Liability Reconsidered: The Impact of Liability Insurance*, 57 Yale L.J. 549 (1948).

31. 2 Parsons, *The Law of Contracts* 304 (2d ed. Boston, 1855); *cf.* I·

Corbin on Contracts 334–337 (St. Paul, 1950). The turn toward the "objective" formula in contract came from the second half of the eighteenth century and in the early part of the nineteenth. Williston, *Mutual Assent in the Formation of Contracts*, 14 Ill. L. Rev. 85, 87 (1919). See Kessler, *Contracts of Adhesion— Some Thoughts about Freedom of Contract*, 43 Col. L. Rev. at 630 (1943); Pound, *op. cit. supra* note 18, at 237, 247, 270.

32. *Oshkosh City Ry. Co.* v. *Winnebago County*, 89 Wis. 435, 437, 61 N.W. 1107 (1895).

33. *Summerfield* v. *Western Union Telegraph Co.*, 87 Wis. 1, 12, 57 N.W. 973, 975 (1894).

34. *Jones* v. *Milwaukee Electric Ry. & L. Co.*, 147 Wis. 427, 435, 133 N.W. 636, 638 (1911).

35. See Livingston Hall, *Strict or Liberal Construction of Penal Statutes*, 48 Harv. L. Rev. 748, 761, 765–767 (1935). Of course, what the text suggests is merely one aspect of policy among the considerations entering into the courts' caution in interpretation of penal statutes. See Jerome Hall, *General Principles of Criminal Law* (Indianapolis, 1947), Ch. II.

36. See, generally, Corwin, *Liberty Against Government* (Baton Rouge, 1948), and 2 *Selected Essays on Constitutional Law* (Chicago, 1938), Ch. I. Aspects of basic changes in property law are discussed in Larkin, *op. cit. supra* note 4, at 141, 148; Scurlock, *Retroactive Legislation Affecting Interests in Land* (Ann Arbor, 1953), pp. 210, 213; Simes, *Historical Background of the Law of Property*, 1 *American Law of Property* 58–60, 63–65 (Boston, 1952); 3 Vernier, *American Family Laws* 34, 167–171, 193 (Stanford, 1935).

37. *Cf.* 2 Dorfman, *The Economic Mind in American Civilization* 630–634, 795, 958–960 (New York, 1946); Hacker, *The Triumph of American Capitalism* (New York, 1940), pp. 317–321, 339–345; Wright, *The Modern Corporation—Twenty Years After*, 19 U. Chi. L. Rev. 662, 665, 667 (1952). Lincoln's position is stated in the letter to Horace Greeley, August 22, 1862, reprinted in 1 *The People Shall Judge* 768–769 (Chicago, 1949).

38. *Fisher* v. *Horicon Iron & Manufacturing Co.*, 10 Wis. 351, 354 (1860); *cf. Newcomb* v. *Smith*, 2 Pinney 131, 140 (Wis. 1849).

39. Brandeis, J., in *Louisville Joint Stock Land Bank* v. *Radford*, 295 U.S. 555, 588 (1935); *cf. Local Loan Co.* v. *Hunt*, 292 U.S. 234, 244 (1934).

40. Waite, C. J., in *Canada Southern Railway Co.* v. *Gebhard*, 109 U.S. 527, 536 (1883). *Cf.* Fuller, *The Background and Techniques of Equity and Bankruptcy Railroad Reorganizations—A Survey*, 7 Law & Contemp. Prob. 377, 378–379 (1940).

41. *Von Baumbach* v. *Bade*, 9 Wis. 559, 583 (1859). Compare the exposition of debtors' exemption laws as a device to conserve essential human resources, in Gov. LaFollette's Veto Message *re* Bill 48A, 47th Wis. Legis., J. Ass., May 3, 1905, pp. 1316–1319.

42. *West River Bridge Co.* v. *Dix*, 6 How. 507 (U.S. 1847).

43. *Providence Bank* v. *Billings*, 4 Pet. 514 (U.S. 1830); *Stone* v. *Mississippi*, 101 U.S. 814 (1880).

44. *Legal Tender Cases*, 12 Wall. 457 (U.S. 1871); *cf. Norman* v. *Baltimore & Ohio Railroad Co.*, 294 U.S. 240 (1935).

45. *Proprietors of the Charles River Bridge* v. *Proprietors of the Warren Bridge,* 11 Pet. 420, 547–548, 552–553 (U.S. 1837).

46. Veto Message of Gov. Jeremiah Rusk, *re* Bill 100S, 35th Wis. Legis., J. Sen., March 21, 1882, pp. 488–490, at 489. Compare, accord, Veto Messages of Gov. LaFollette, *re* Bill 371A, 45th Wis. Legis., J. Ass., April 2, 1901, p. 723 ("The unqualified existence and continuance of the grant for the entire period might hamper and even stifle the growth of other great and paramount interests to the detriment of the public welfare."); *re* Bill 25S, 46th Wis. Legis., J. Sen., May 11, 1903, pp. 1038–1039.

47. *Cf.* Smith, *A Dangerous Freedom* (Philadelphia, 1954), Chs. VI–IX; Wertenbaker, *The Puritan Oligarchy* (New York, 1947), pp. 339–345; Myers, *Blue Laws,* 3 Enc. Soc. Sci. 600 (14 vols. New York, 1930); Vincent, *Sumptuary Legislation,* 4 *id.* 464 (1934).

48. *Cf.* Chafee, *Free Speech in the United States* (Cambridge, 1942), p. 437; Miller, *Crisis in Freedom* (Boston, 1951), pp. 193, 221, 226–227, 230; Woodward, *Reunion and Reaction* (Boston, 1951), pp. 13, 15, 208, 211–212, 214–215.

49. See Spengler, *Laissez Faire and Intervention: A Potential Source of Historical Error,* J. Pol. Ec. 438, 440 (1949).

CHAPTER II

1. Bancroft, *The Office of the People,* in *Literary and Historical Miscellanies* (New York, 1855), p. 408.

2. Jefferson, *Notes on the State of Virginia,* in Padover, *The Complete Jefferson* (New York, 1943; Original, 1782), p. 668; see Merriam and Bourgin, *Jefferson as a Planner of National Resources,* 53 Ethics 284, 286, 289 (1943). Whatever his hesitation on constitutional grounds, Jefferson saw the Louisiana Purchase as an essential use of the power of the central government to shape the conditions of future safety and independence for the United States. See 2 Adams, *History of the United States During the Administration of Thomas Jefferson* 84–85 (Boni, ed. New York, 1930).

3. 1 Reports of the Secretary of the Treasury 78, 93 (Washington, 1837); compare his opinion on the constitutionality of the Bank of the United States, 4 *id.* 105.

4. Annals of Congress, 18th Cong., 1st Sess. (2 vols. Washington, 1856), Vol. I, pp. 1022, 1035; *cf.* Report of Select Committee on Memorial of The Milwaukee & Waukesha Railroad Co., 3rd Wis. Legis., J. Ass., Jan. 22, 1850, pp. 103–108, at 106.

5. Message of Gov. Dewey, Jan. 11, 1849, 1st Wis. Legis., J. Sen., pp. 9–32, at 31; *cf.* Message of Gov. Farwell, Jan. 13, 1853, 6th Wis. Legis., J. Sen., pp. 11–18, at 13; Message of Gov. Bashford, Sept. 3, 1855, 9th Wis. Legis. (Adj. Sess.), J. Sen., pp. 926–931, at 929; Veto Message of Gov. Bashford, Oct. 7, 1855, *id.,* pp. 1143–1148, at 1144.

6. 1 Stimson, *American Statute Law* 21–23 (Boston, 1886); Lewis, *Law of Eminent Domain* (Chicago, 1888), p. i; Levy, *Chief Justice Shaw and the Formative Period of American Railroad Law,* 51 Col. L. Rev. 327, 328, n. 7 (1951).

7. Redfield, C.J., in *Thorpe* v. *Rutland and Burlington Railroad Co.,* 27 Vt. 140, 149 (1854); *cf.* Shaw, C.J., in *Commonwealth* v. *Alger,* 7 Cush. 53 (Mass. 1851). On the middle-class philosophy of effort to shape circumstances, see 2 Tocqueville, *Democracy in America* 33–34, 136–139 (Bradley, ed. New York, 1945). On the Constitution as a framework for growth, see Marshall, C.J., in *McCulloch* v. *Maryland,* 4 Wheat. 316, 401, 407 (U.S. 1819); Waite, C.J., in *Pensacola Telegraph Co.* v. *Western Union Telegraph Co.,* 96 U.S. 1, 9 (1877); *cf.* Cahn, ed., *Supreme Court and Supreme Law* (Bloomington, 1954), pp. 55–58.

8. Colonial loyalty laws are discussed in Hurst, *Treason in the United States,* 58 Harv. L. Rev. 226 (1945); social regulations, in Boorstin, *The Genius of American Politics* (Chicago, 1953), Ch. II; Myers, *Blue Laws,* 3 Encyc. Soc. Sci. 600 (New York, 1930), and Vincent, *Sumptuary Legislation,* 14 *id.* 464 (New York, 1934); economic regulation, in Hartz, *Economic Policy and Democratic Thought: Pennsylvania, 1776–1860* (Cambridge, 1948), pp. 4–9, and Johnson and Krooss, *The Origins and Development of the American Economy* (New York, 1953), p. 336; *cf.* Adler, *Business Jurisprudence,* 28 Harv. L. Rev. 135 (1914); 2 *Selected Essays on Constitutional Law* 436 (Chicago, 1938); Read, *Mercantilism: The Old English Pattern of a Controlled Economy,* in Read, ed., *The Constitution Reconsidered* (New York, 1938), pp. 63, 76.

9. *The Federalist* (Lodge, ed. New York, 1888), No. 10 (Madison), p. 51.

10. Calhoun, *A Disquisition on Government,* 1 *Works* 12, 25 (New York, 1851).

11. *Scott* v. *Sandford,* 19 How. 393 (U.S. 1857) was a disastrous effort by the Supreme Court to affect the political environment in the interest of an already outdated balance of power. The Court's failure stands as one of our prime lessons in the hazards of exceeding the limits of effective legal action. But the decision's failure was also some evidence of the strength of those currents in the century's policy which sought to create conditions favorable to the maximum release of energy.

12. *Gibbons* v. *Ogden,* 9 Wheat. 1 (U.S. 1824); *Brown* v. *Maryland,* 12 Wheat. 419 (U.S. 1827). The concurring opinion of Johnson, J., in *Gibbons* v. *Ogden,* 9 Wheat. at 222, which rested on a simple finding of state invasion of a field which Johnson thought exclusively committed to Congress, emphasizes with what deliberation Marshall chose a more complicated doctrine.

13. *Gibbons* v. *Ogden,* 9 Wheat. 1, 195 (U.S. 1824).

14. *Id.* at 197.

15. *Welton* v. *Missouri,* 91 U.S. 275, 279–280, 282 (1875); *cf. Walling* v. *Michigan,* 116 U.S. 446 (1886); *Robbins* v. *Shelby County Taxing District,* 120 U.S. 489 (1887).

16. *Reading Railroad Co.* v. *Pennsylvania,* 15 Wall. 232, 280 (U.S. 1872).

17. *Wabash, St. Louis & Pacific Railway Co.* v. *Illinois,* 118 U.S. 557, 572–573 (1886).

18. Henderson, *The Position of Foreign Corporations in American Constitu-*

tional Law (Cambridge, 1918), Chs. III, IV, VI, VII, and especially pp. 132–133. *Cf.* Stone, C.J., in *International Shoe Co.* v. *Washington,* 326 U.S. 314 (1945).

19. *Pennsylvania* v. *The Wheeling and Belmont Bridge Co.,* 18 How. 421 (U.S. 1855); see *Gilman* v. *Philadelphia,* 3 Wall. 713, 732 (U.S. 1865).

20. 14 Stat. 66; see Cadman, *The Corporation in New Jersey* (Cambridge, 1949), pp. 54–60; 2 Dorfman, *The Economic Mind in American Civilization* 801 (New York, 1946); Fairman, *Mr. Justice Miller and the Supreme Court, 1862–1890* (Cambridge, 1939), p. 310; Henderson, *op. cit. supra* note 18, at 112–113; Prentice, *The Federal Power over Carriers and Corporations* (New York, 1907), pp. 95, 209.

21. *California* v. *Pacific Railroad Companies,* 127 U.S. 39 (1887); see Bradley, J., dissenting, in *Railroad Co.* v. *Peniston,* 18 Wall. 5, 47–48 (U.S. 1873). *Cf. Luxton* v. *North River Bridge Co.,* 153 U.S. 525 (1894).

22. Fairman, *op. cit. supra* note 20, at 310; Prentice, *op. cit. supra* note 20, at 152; see, *e.g.,* Wis. L. 1865, Ch. 485.

23. *Pensacola Telegraph Co.* v. *Western Union Telegraph Co.,* 96 U.S. 1, 10 (1877).

24. See remarks of Sen. Sherman, Cong. Globe, 39th Cong., 1st Sess., 3481, June 29, 1866.

25. *Shreveport Cases,* 234 U.S. 342 (1914).

26. Note 17 *supra;* see 1 Sharfman, *The Interstate Commerce Commission* 19 (New York, 1931). In effect, Congress "licensed" the broader reach of state Prohibition policy when, in the Webb-Kenyon Act, it forbade interstate transportation of liquor intended to be used in violation of the law of any state. But clearly it was the peculiarities of the liquor traffic, and not any general issue of the national free trade area, which was deemed to be involved. See Act of March 1, 1913, 37 Stat. 699; Veto Message of President Taft, 49 Cong. Rec. (pt. 5) 4291, 63rd Cong., 1st Sess. (1917); *Clark Distilling Co.* v. *Western Maryland Railway Co.,* 242 U.S. 311 (1917). On trends which produced a rising twentieth-century demand for Congress to take a more active role in policing state encroachments on interstate commerce, see Truitt, *Interstate Trade Barriers in the United States,* 8 Law & Contemp. Prob. 209, 210–212 (1941).

27. Compare Field, J., in *Welton* v. *Missouri,* note 15 *supra,* with Story, J., dissenting, in *Mayor etc. of the City of New York* v. *Miln,* 11 Pet. 102, 160 (U.S. 1837).

28. *Hammer* v. *Dagenhart,* 247 U.S. 251 (1918); *Bailey* v. *Drexel Furniture Co.,* 259 U.S. 20 (1922).

29. The picture so carefully put together for the pre-1824 period, by Professor Abel, tallies with the later situation. See Abel, *Commerce Regulation Before Gibbons v. Ogden,* 25 No. Car. L. Rev. 121 (1947); *cf.* Hartz, *op. cit. supra* note 8, at 204–218; Wis. Rev. Stat., 1878, Chs. 51, 52, 53, 66, 67, 68, 70, and Titles XVIII, XIX.

30. See *Cooley* v. *The Board of Wardens of the Port of Philadelphia,* 12 How. 299 (U.S. 1851); *Gilman* v. *Philadelphia,* 3 Wall. 713 (U.S. 1865); *Woodruff* v. *Parham,* 8 Wall. 123 (U.S. 1868); *Smith* v. *Alabama,* 124 U.S. 465 (1888). Especially striking is *Railroad Co.* v. *Maryland,* 21 Wall. 456 (U.S.

1874), in view of its overruling by *Wabash, St. Louis & Pacific Railway Co.* v. *Illinois,* 118 U.S. 557 (1886).

31. See *Munn* v. *Illinois,* 94 U.S. 113, 134 (1877); *Railroad Commission Cases,* 116 U.S. 307 (1886); *cf.* Corwin, *Liberty Against Government* (Baton Rouge, 1948), Ch. IV; *cf.* also, however, Corwin, *The Twilight of the Supreme Court* (New Haven, 1934), pp. 48–49. It is not until late in the century that due process is definitely involved as a basis for invalidating legislation discriminating against interstate commerce or based on an insufficient ground of local interest in the regulated transaction. *Cf. Minnesota* v. *Barber,* 136 U.S. 313 (1890).

32. Henderson, *op. cit. supra* note 18, Ch. VI; see his discussion of the dissent of Field, J., in the *Pensacola Telegraph Co.* case, *id.,* 115.

33. See *Jensen* v. *Board of Supervisors of Polk County,* 47 Wis. 298, 308–314, 2 N.W. 320, 327–332 (1879); *cf.* Angell and Durfee, *Law of Highways* (2d ed. Boston, 1868), pp. 297–298; Elliott, *Law of Roads and Streets* (3d ed. Indianapolis, 1911), Ch. XIX. Analogous policy is expressed in Wisconsin Gov. Harvey's Message of April 5, 1862, vetoing Bill 62S (to donate swamplands to the counties wherein they lay), 15th Wis. Legis., J. Sen., pp. 809–819.

34. Dykstra, *Legislation and Change,* 1950 Wis. L. Rev. 523; Handlin and Handlin, *Commonwealth: Massachusetts, 1774–1861* (New York, 1947), pp. 76, 82. The policies in the background of such legislation are brought out in the Veto Message of Gov. Farwell, June 6, 1853, 6th Wis. Legis., J. Sen., pp. 815–817; and in Majority and Minority Reports of the Select Committee on Bill 352A (repeal of the charter of The Black River Improvement Co.), 20th Wis. Legis., J. Ass., April 8, 1867, p. 1106, and App., pp. 1266–1272. See 1 Farnham, *The Law of Waters* 384–392 (Rochester, 1904).

35. 1 Bonbright, *Valuation of Property* 634–645 (New York, 1937); Groves, *Financing Government* (New York, 1939), pp. 279–287; Snider, *The Taxation of the Gross Receipts of Railways in Wisconsin* (Publications, Am. Ec. Ass'n., 3rd Ser., Vol. XII, No. 4. 1906), pp. 1–11; Brown and Hurst, *Perils of the Test Case,* 1949 Wis. L. Rev. 26.

36. *Town of Pacific Junction* v. *Dyer,* 64 Iowa 38, 19 N.W. 862 (1884); *Brooks* v. *Mangan,* 86 Mich. 576, 49 N.W. 633 (1891); *State* v. *Whitcom,* 122 Wis. 110, 114, 99 N.W. 468, 469 (1904) ("Our statute relating to the licensing and punishing of peddlers and transient merchants. . . . is an edifice of composite architecture, made up of a series of portholed turrets for offense against the obnoxious, and sheltered corridors to shield the favorites of the successive legislatures which have contributed to the conglomerate now under consideration."). See the review of the history of policy in this field, in *Whipple* v. *City of South Milwaukee,* 218 Wis. 395, 261 N.W. 235 (1935), and in Comment, 41 Yale L.J. 227 (1932).

37. 1 Hunt, *Lives of American Merchants* 570 (2 vols. New York, 1856–1858). See a similar contemporary description of middle-western attitudes in the first stage of railroad growth, quoted in Taylor, *The Farmers' Movement, 1620–1920* (New York, 1953), pp. 146–147. *Cf.* Cochran and Miller, *The Age of Enterprise* (New York, 1943), pp. 77–80; 1 Dorfman, *op. cit. supra* note 20, at 381–382, 622–625; Hartz, *op. cit. supra* note 8, at 11, 64, 75.

38. Message of Gov. Barstow, Jan. 12, 1854, 7th Wis. Legis., J. Sen., pp. 11–26, at 22–23.

39. 2 Dorfman, *op. cit. supra* note 20, at 624, 625; compare policy expressions in the Wisconsin documents cited note 34 *supra*.

40. Message of Gov. Farwell, Jan. 15, 1852, 5th Wis. Legis., J. Sen., pp. 10–26, at 22, 25, 26; *cf.* Message of Gov. Barstow, Jan. 12, 1854, 7th Wis. Legis., J. Sen., pp. 11–26, at 24; Message of Gov. Bashford, Sept. 3, 1855, 9th Wis. Legis. (Adj. Sess.), J. Sen., pp. 926–931, at 929. Note the changing, more cautious tone in Message of Gov. Randall, Jan. 15, 1858, 11th Wis. Legis., J. Sen., pp. 19–60, at 43. On the general enthusiasm for the moral and libertarian implications of a liberal public land policy, see Smith, *Virgin Land* (Cambridge, 1950), pp. 123–144; on the emphasis on the economic base of a new kind of society, *id.*, 155–164.

41. Hibbard, *A History of the Public Land Policies* (New York, 1939), p. 138; Gates, *Fifty Million Acres* (Ithaca, 1954), pp. 4, 9–13. Wis. Rev. Stat., 1878, secs. 196–201, express the characteristic legislative stress on sale to actual settlers.

42. See Smith, *Economic Aspects of the Second Bank of the United States* (Cambridge, 1953), pp. 62, 143. Compare the expression of a like attitude on a state level, in the "Suffolk System" which controlled the circulating medium in New England in the 1830's and 1840's, Handlin and Handlin, *op. cit. supra* note 34, at 181–182; and in the creation of the Bank of the State of Missouri, Primm, *Economic Policy in the Development of a Western State: Missouri, 1820–1860* (Cambridge, 1954), pp. 28–31.

43. Register of Debates in Congress, 21st Cong., 2d Sess., Sen. (Washington, 1831), Vol. VII, pp. 50, 51. This distrust of banking power was expressed in Benton's home state's policy of putting the central bank function in the hands of a state institution. Primm, *op. cit. supra* note 42, at 28–29. *Cf.* Brown, *The Making of the Wisconsin Constitution*, 1949 Wis. L. Rev. 648, 676–681; 1952 *id.* 23, 48–51.

44. 2 Dorfman, *op. cit. supra* note 20, at 596, 618–619, 771; Hacker, *The Triumph of American Capitalism* (New York, 1940), pp. 330–335, 365–368; Hartz, *op. cit. supra* note 8, at 49, 53–55, 66–69, 90, 196, 254–258; Henderson, *op. cit supra* note 18, at 45–48; Brown, *op. cit. supra* note 43, especially 1952 Wis. L. Rev. at 50–51. See Wis. L. 1852, Ch. 479, and Andersen, *A Century of Banking in Wisconsin* (Madison, 1954), pp. 19, 21, 22–24. On the impact of the 10 per cent federal tax, see Andersen, pp. 51–52.

45. Report on Manufactures, Dec., 1791, *op. cit. supra* note 3, at 88; *cf.* Clay, Speech of Aug. 3, 1830, on "The American System," 1 *Life and Speeches of the Hon. Henry Clay* 647–648 (Mallory, ed. New York, 1857); 1 Dorfman, *op. cit. supra* note 20, at 325, 385, 390; 2 *id.* 532, 567–569.

46. 3 Dorfman, *op. cit. supra* note 20, at 9, 51–52; Handlin, *The Uprooted* (Boston, 1951), Chs. I, II, III, XI, and *The American People in the Twentieth Century* (Cambridge, 1954), Chs. I, III, IV; Hibbard, *op. cit. supra* note 41, at 138–139, 141–143; *The Passenger Cases*, 7 How. 283 (U.S. 1848). Typical reflections of state policy may be seen in the Messages of Wisconsin Governors: *e.g.*, Gov. Barstow, Jan. 11, 1855, 9th Wis. Legis., J. Sen., pp. 12–36, at

33–35; Gov. Fairchild, Jan. 10, 1867, 20th Wis. Legis., J. Sen., pp. 13–34, at 22, Jan. 9, 1868, 21st Wis. Legis., J. Sen., pp. 11–26, at 21, and Jan. 14, 1869, 22d Wis. Legis., J. Sen., pp. 13–29, at 23; Gov. Taylor, Jan. 15, 1874, 27th Wis. Legis., J. Ass., App., pp. 3–26, at 10; Gov. Ludington, Jan. 13, 1876, 29th Wis. Legis., 1 Public Documents 1–15, at 8.

47. *The Federalist*, No. 3 (Jay), pp. 12, 15; No. 30 (Hamilton), pp. 174, 177, 179; No. 80 (Hamilton), pp. 494, 495, 500; Hamilton, First Report on the Public Credit, Jan., 1790, p. 3; Fairman, *op. cit. supra* note 20, Ch. IX; Frank, *Historical Bases of the Federal Judicial System*, 13 Law & Contemp. Prob. 3, 13–14, 24–27 (1948); Johnson and Krooss, *op. cit. supra* note 8, at 132–133, 292–293.

48. Hibbard, *op. cit. supra* note 41, Ch. I.

49. Message of Gov. Barstow, Jan. 11, 1855, 9th Wis. Legis., J. Sen., pp. 12–36, at 27–28; *cf.* Clay, *loc. cit.* note 45 *supra*. See Current, *Pine Logs and Politics* (Madison, 1950), pp. 46, 60, 98–100, on the strength of the pork barrel policy; and note the Veto Message of Gov. Harvey, cited note 33 *supra*, reflecting the pork barrel problem as between the state and its counties.

50. On the nineteenth-century experience in direct grant and investment of public funds and the lending of public credit, see Cochran and Miller, *op. cit. supra* note 37, at 41–42, 50–51; Corwin, *The Twilight of the Supreme Court*, pp. 156–177; Fairman, *op. cit. supra* note 20, Ch. IX; Hartz, *op. cit. supra* note 8, Chs. III, IV; on the public purpose doctrine, Hartz, *loc. cit.*, pp. 113–126, and Jacobs, *Law Writers and the Constitution* (Berkeley and Los Angeles, 1954), Chs. IV, V, especially pp. 129, 134, 157–159. On the twentieth-century trend, see Jacobs, pp. 150–156; *Green v. Frazier*, 253 U.S. 233 (1920); *Massachusetts v. Mellon*, 262 U.S. 447 (1923); *Steward Machine Co. v. Davis*, and *Helvering v. Davis*, 301 U.S. 518, 619 (1937); Corwin, *loc. cit.*, Ch. IV. The Wisconsin record makes a revealing case history. The Constitution of 1848 set strict limits on state debt and participation in works of internal improvement, which the state Supreme Court strictly enforced, but which were relaxed by constitutional amendments. Brown, *The Making of the Wisconsin Constitution*, 1949 Wis. L. Rev. at 673–676, and 1952 *id.* at 45–48. On the other hand, the Wisconsin constitutional convention omitted a proposed firm ban on local government debt, in favor of a general mandate to the legislature to exercise surveillance of municipal finance. 1949 Wis. L. Rev. at 691; 1952 *id.* at 43. *Cf.* Hunt, *Law and Early Wisconsin Railroads* (Unpublished S.J.D. Thesis, on deposit in the Law Library, University of Wisconsin, Madison, 1952), Chs. I, III, V; Knight, *Subsidization of Industry in Forty Selected Cities in Wisconsin, 1930–1946* (Univ. Wis. Bull., Commerce Studies, Vol. I, No. 2. Madison, 1947).

51. Hubbell, J., in *Newcomb v. Smith*, 3 Pinney 131, 140 (Wis. 1849); compare the stress on the delegation of power involved, in the dissent of Larrabee, J., *id.*; *cf. Head v. Amoskeag Manufacturing Co.*, 113 U.S. 9 (1885).

52. *Pratt v. Brown*, 3 Wis. 603, 610 (1854); *cf. Fisher v. Horicon Iron & Manufacturing Co.*, 10 Wis. 351 (1860). On the general recognition of the policy of delegating eminent domain powers in aid of capital development, see Cadman, *op. cit. supra* note 20, at 223; Dodd, *American Business Corporations. until 1860* (Cambridge, 1954), pp. 128, 158–161, 404; Handlin and Handlin,

op. cit. supra note 34, at 116. On sensitivity to the extent of the power of compulsion so delegated, see Handlin and Handlin, *loc. cit.*, p. 222; Hartz, *op. cit. supra* note 8, at 70, 76, 248; 2 Kirkland, *Men, Cities and Transportation* 332 (Cambridge, 1952); and, generally, 1 Bonbright, *op. cit. supra* note 35, at 411–412, 448; Lenhoff, *Development of the Concept of Eminent Domain*, 42 Col. L. Rev. 596, 600, 615, 637–638 (1942); 2 Orgel, *Valuation under the Law of Eminent Domain* 252–265 (2d ed. 2 vols. Charlottesville, 1953).

53. Cf. *Noesen v. Port Washington*, 37 Wis. 168 (1875).

54. *Railroad Commission Cases*, 116 U.S. 307, 330 (1886); *Georgia Railroad and Banking Co. v. Smith*, 128 U.S. 174, 179–182 (1888); cf. *Sands v. Manistee River Improvement Co.*, 123 U.S. 288, 294 (1887); Brandeis, J., in *The New England Divisions Case*, 261 U.S. 184, 196 (1923); Landis, Comm'r, dissenting, in *United Air Lines, Inc.–Western Air Lines, Inc., Acquisition of Air Carrier Property*, 8 Ec. Dec. C.A.B. 298, 325 (1947); Jaffe, *Law Making by Private Groups*, 51 Harv. L. Rev. 201, 218 (1937); 2 Kirkland, *op. cit. supra* note 52, at 320. That sovereign power was delegated was particularly clear with regard to toll rights under river improvement charters in Wisconsin, where a public purpose was found, but the constitutional ban on state participation in works of internal improvement was deemed to prevent direct state action to remove obstructions to navigation. See *Wisconsin River Improvement Co. v. Manson*, 43 Wis. 584, 593–594 (1877). To avoid "oppressive" results, the court would construe an improvement statute as granting toll rights only to very specifically indicated grantees. *Sellers v. The Union Lumbering Co.*, 39 Wis. 525, 528 (1876). On the grant of toll rights as resembling a delegation of a taxing power, see Minority Report, Select Committee on Bill 223S (Black River Improvement Co. charter), 10th Wis. Legis., J. Ass., March 3, 1857, p. 749; "memorials" against allegedly oppressive rates of the Apple River Log Driving Co., 26th Wis. Legis., J. Ass., Feb. 11, 1873, p. 304, Feb. 17, p. 394, and Feb. 19, p. 425; Message of Gov. R. M. LaFollette, 46th Wis. Legis., J. Ass., Jan. 15, 1903, p. 21, at 35, 41, 56, 69, and his Special Message of April 29, 1903, *id.*, App., pp. 1415, 1425, 1426, 1437; cf. Report, Committee on Incorporations *re* Bill 14S (repeal of Kilbourn Dam franchise), 26th Wis. Legis., J. Ass., Feb. 18, 1873, p. 229; Report of Conference between Joint Committee on Assessment and Collection of Taxes, and Representatives of Various Railroads, 46th Wis. Legis., J. Sen., Feb. 18, 1903, pp. 312–349, at 342 (railroad tax exemption as aid to road's capacity to borrow on its lands).

55. Benton, *loc. cit. supra* note 43. Cf. Andersen, *op. cit. supra* note 44, at 35, 58–59.

56. Cf. 2 Tocqueville, *op. cit. supra* note 7, at 106–111; and see Handlin and Handlin, *op. cit. supra* note 34, at 105; Dodd, *op. cit. supra* note 52, at 159–160.

57. Warren, *The Making of the Constitution* (Boston, 1928), pp. 590–598.

58. The contemporary policy favoring reservation of a power to amend or repeal franchises is stated in representative fashion by Veto Messages of Gov. Rusk, March 21, 1882, 35th Wis. Legis., J. Sen., pp. 488–490; compare his general Message of Jan. 11, 1883, 36th Wis. Legis., J. Ass., pp. 11–25, at 24, and, generally, Note, 31 Col. L. Rev. 1163 (1931); 2 *Selected Essays on Constitu-*

tional Law 352 (Chicago, 1938). The classic statements of the policy grounds for the strict interpretation of special charters are contained in *Proprietors of the Charles River Bridge* v. *Proprietors of the Warren Bridge*, 11 Pet. 420 (U.S. 1837), and in *Ohio Life Insurance & Trust Co.* v. *Debolt*, 16 How. 415 (U.S. 1854); on the police power and the contracts clause, see cases cited, note 54 *supra*. On the preference of railroad development over older transport, see the *Charles River Bridge* case *supra*, and *Pennsylvania* v. *Wheeling and Belmont Bridge Co.*, 18 How. 421 (U.S. 1856).

59. Brown, *op. cit. supra* note 43, 1949 Wis. L. Rev. at 671, 673, and 1952 *id.* at 52–53; Farnam, *Chapters in the History of Social Legislation in the United States to 1860* (Day, ed. Washington, 1938), Ch. XI; compare Ch. I of these essays, notes 29, 30, 31.

60. *Cf.* Bogart, *Economic History of the American People* (2d ed. New York, 1938), pp. 394, 395, 397, 398.

61. *Cf.* Hacker and Kendrick, *The United States Since 1865* (rev. ed. New York, 1936), pp. 150–163; Fairman, *op. cit. supra* note 20, Ch. XI; Hunt, *op. cit. supra* note 50; Merk, *Economic History of Wisconsin During the Civil War Decade* (Madison, 1916), pp. 238–270; Winslow, *The Story of a Great Court* (Chicago, 1912), pp. 167–179.

62. Beard and Beard, *The American Leviathan* (New York, 1930), pp. 360–370; Gates, *op. cit. supra* note 41, at 5, 9–10, 51–52, 224; Hacker and Kendrick, *op. cit. supra* note 61, at 206–207.

63. The remarks quoted are contained and discussed in Brooks Adams' introductory chapter to his volume of the essays of his brother, Henry, entitled *The Degradation of the Democratic Dogma* (New York, 1920), pp. 27, 31.

64. Report, Committee on Schools, Jan. 10, 1842, 3rd Wis. Legis., 2d Sess., J. Ass., pp. 89–97, at 93, 94, 96, 97 (italics in original).

65. See, *e.g.*, Communication from Hiram Barber, Dec. 18, 1848, 2d Wis. Legis., J. Sen., pp. 686–694, at 689; Reports, Committee on Agriculture and Manufactures, Feb. 3, 1858, 11th Wis. Legis., J. Sen., pp. 232–238, at 235, and Feb. 25, 1863, 16th Wis. Legis., J. Sen., p. 359; Report, Select Committee *re* Bill 191A, Feb. 13, 1867, 20th Wis. Legis., J. Ass., pp. 283–286.

CHAPTER III

1. U.S. Bureau of the Census, *Historical Statistics of the United States, 1789–1945* (Washington, D.C., 1949), pp. 9–11, 25, 33, 63, 280–282; Holcombe, *The Middle Classes in American Politics* (Cambridge, 1940), p. 198; Johnson and Krooss, *The Origins and Development of the American Economy* (New York, 1953), pp. 164, 190, 192, 306, 312; 2 Morison and Commager, *The Growth of the American Republic* (3rd ed. New York, 1942), Chs. V, VI, VII; Schlesinger, *The Rise of the City, 1878–1898* (New York, 1938), Ch. III; Soule, *Economic Forces in American History* (New York, 1952), pp. 104, 157, 159, 206, 210; Still, *Milwaukee* (Madison, 1948), pp. 257–259; Stocking and Wat-

kins, *Monopoly and Free Enterprise* (New York, 1951), pp. 23–24, 32; Thorp and Crowder, *The Structure of Industry*, TNEC Monograph No. 27 (Washington, D.C., 1941), pp. 5–7, 12, 18, 231–234.

2. 2 Bryce, *The American Commonwealth* 407 (New York and London, 1889). Compare Henry George's summary of the vision of the times against which he saw men measure their frustration, in *Progress and Poverty* (50th anniversary ed. New York, 1932), pp. 4–5; see Horney, *The Neurotic Personality of Our Time* (New York, 1937), pp. 288–289.

3. Quoted in 3 Parrington, *The Beginnings of Critical Realism in America, 1860–1920* 297 (New York, 1930); *cf.* Beer, *Hanna* (New York, 1929), pp. 88–91, 114–119; Dulles, *Labor in America* (New York, 1949), pp. 133, 136, 142, 145; McConnell, *The Decline of Agrarian Democracy* (Berkeley and Los Angeles, 1953), pp. 6, 11; Taylor, *The Farmers' Movement* (New York, 1953), p. 233.

4. See the estimates of the meaning of the popular response to *Progress and Poverty*, in Beer, *op. cit. supra* note 3, at 255; Chamberlain, *Farewell to Reform* (New York, 1932), pp. 45, 61, 247; 3 Dorfman, *The Economic Mind in American Civilization* 141 (New York, 1949); 2 Steffens, *Autobiography* 475 (1 vol. ed. New York, 1931). The audience attracted by the "muck rakers" also attested the growing interest in social process and the collection and analysis of facts about it. See Commager, *The American Mind* (New Haven, 1950), pp. 328–335; 3 Dorfman, 1 *op. cit. supra*, p. 102.

5. See, generally, Clark, *Social Control of Business* (Chicago, 1926), pp. 132–139; Freund, *Standards of American Legislation* (Chicago, 1917), pp. 50–51, 54, 70, 71, 117, 123–128; Holmes, *Law in Science—Science in Law*, in *Collected Legal Papers* (New York, 1921), pp. 210, 230; 1 Nims, *Unfair Competition and Trade-Marks* (4th ed. 2 vols. New York, 1947), Ch. XII. Growth of recognition of the vulnerability of the average man before the compulsions of our contract-organized society is discussed in Drucker, *Structure of the Enterprise: Economic, Governmental, Social*, 44 Ill. L. Rev. 769 (1950); Kessler, *Contracts of Adhesion—Some Thoughts about Freedom of Contract*, 43 Col. L. Rev. 629, 632 ff. (1943); Radin, *Contract Obligation and the Human Will, id.*, 575, 579–581. Law-imposed standardization in contract terms was partly a response to this recognition; standardization might be used to help equalize parties' positions if the law set the terms on which it was done. *Cf.* Isaacs, *The Standardization of Contracts*, 27 Yale L.J. 34, 38, 47 (1917); Kessler, *Corbin on Contracts: Formation of Contracts*, 61 Yale L.J. 1092, 1098 (1952).

6. *Dodge* v. *Ford Motor Co.*, 204 Mich. 459, 507, 170 N.W. 668, 684 (1919); see Nevins, *Ford* (New York, 1954), pp. 575–576. On the standing of private and public suitors, see, *e.g.*, Walsh, *Equity* (Chicago, 1930), p. 209, and Beuscher, *Public Representation in Private Litigation Involving Administrative Rules*, 1942 Wis. L. Rev. 355. Compare Freund's comments on the main focus of common law on conflicts of private interest, *op. cit. supra* note 5, at 69.

7. Nevins, ed., *America Through British Eyes* (New York, 1948), pp. 356, 358. The limited scope of nineteenth-century economics is appraised in Kapp, *The Social Costs of Private Enterprise* (Cambridge, 1950), Ch. I; Schumpeter, *History of Economic Analysis* (New York, 1954), pp. 886, 889, 896–897, 985,

1070–1073. 1 Bonbright, *Valuation of Property* 40, 43, 63, 65 (New York, 1937), discusses the law's focus on exchange or market value as a concept natural for our society.

8. 2 Tocqueville, *Democracy in America* 157 (Bradley, ed. 2 vols. New York, 1948). On the state's reserved powers over contracts, see in the present essays, Ch. I, notes 6–8, and Ch. II, note 54. Tentative steps toward broader views of social cost and structural factors in situations may be seen in 7th Biennial Report, Wisconsin Bureau of Labor, Census and Industrial Statistics (1896), 43rd Wis. Legis., 2 Public Documents 145; and in Report, Wisconsin Forestry Commission (1898), 44th Wis. Legis., 2 Public Documents 13–19.

9. See the appraisal by Frankfurter, J., dissenting, in *Panhandle Eastern Pipe Line Co.* v. *Michigan Public Service Commission*, 341 U.S. 329, 340 (1951), and the comments thereon by Freund in Cahn, ed., *Supreme Court and Supreme Law* (Bloomington, 1954), pp. 96–105. *Cf.* Final Report of the Executive Secretary, Temporary National Economic Commission on the Concentration of Economic Power in the United States, 77th Cong., 1st Sess. (Washington, D.C., 1941), pp. 143–163.

10. Gates, *The Wisconsin Pine Lands of Cornell University* (Ithaca, 1943), pp. 245–246; *cf. id.* 46–48, and Ch. IV; see, also by Gates, his *Land Policy and Tenancy in the Prairie States*, 1 J. Ec. Hist. 60, 73, 77, 82 (1941), and his *Role of the Land Speculator in Western Development*, 66 Pa. Mag. of Hist. & Biog. 314, 322–323, 326, 332 (1942); *cf.* 1 Schafer, *Wisconsin Domesday Book: Town Studies* 10 (Madison, 1924), and his *Wisconsin Lead Region* (Madison, 1932), pp. 151–154. Hibbard, *History of the Public Land Policies* (New York, 1939), discusses the realization on railroad lands, at pp. 261–263, and notes the concentration of holdings in some areas as a result of the mode of disposition; see also his Chs. XXI and XXIV on the significance of land classification. Concerning the significance of the release of state land claims to the federal government, see Merriam and Bourgin, *Jefferson as a Planner of National Resources*, 53 Ethics 284, 285, 291 (1943).

11. Patterson, *Federal Debt-Management Policies, 1865–1879* (Durham, 1954), pp. 204, 211–214. *Cf.* Cochran and Miller, *The Age of Enterprise* (New York, 1943), pp. 105–106, 112, 118; Frank, *Recapturing War Profit—A Civil War Experience*, 1947 Wis. L. Rev. 212; Groves, *Financing Government* (New York, 1939), pp. 154–155, 330, 340; Hacker, *The Triumph of American Capitalism* (New York, 1940), pp. 361–368; 2 Morison and Commager, *op. cit. supra* note 1, at 65–68; Soule, *op. cit. supra* note 1, at 217–218; U.S. Bureau of the Census, *op. cit. supra* note 1, at 303, 304, 306.

12. The quoted expressions of typical mid-century optimism are, respectively, from Report, Assembly Committee on Incorporations, March 2, 1866, *re* Bill 9S (charter of Columbia Manufacturing Co.), 19th Wis. Legis., J. Ass., pp. 454–457, at 455 (but *cf.* Report, Senate Committee on Incorporations, Jan. 25, 1866, *id.*, J. Sen., pp. 135–137, at 136); and Preliminary Report on the Eighth Census, 1860 (Washington, D.C., 1862), p. 59. On Standard Oil and Rockefeller accumulations, see 2 Nevins, *John D. Rockefeller* 195, 719 (New York, 1940); on Carnegie, 2 Morison and Commager, *op. cit. supra* note 1, at 133–134, Hacker, *op. cit. supra* note 11, at 418, 421, 423, and Johnson and Krooss, *op. cit. supra* note 1, at 189; on Ford, Nevins, *Ford* (New York, 1954),

pp. 490, 647, 649–650; on the insurance companies, North, *Capital Accumulation in Life Insurance between the Civil War and the Investigations of 1905*, in Miller, ed., *Men in Business* (Cambridge, 1952), pp. 238, 239–240, 252; on the investment bankers, the Report of the Subcommittee of the House Committee on Banking and Currency, H.R. Doc. No. 504, 62d Cong., 2d Sess. (Washington, D.C., 1913), and Hacker and Zahler, *The United States in the 20th Century* (New York, 1952), pp. 73–77.

13. Schumpeter, *op. cit. supra* note 7, at 945; *cf.* Raushenbush, *The Corporation: An Institutional Factor in Modern History*, in Ware, ed., *The Cultural Approach to History* (New York, 1940), p. 167. 1 Sharfman, *The Interstate Commerce Commission* (New York, 1931), Chs. I, II, portrays the limited scope of the first generation of national railroad regulation; on the state experience, see Buck, *The Granger Movement* (Cambridge, 1913), Chs. IV, V, VI. On post–Civil War tax policy, see, further, 3 Dorfman, *op. cit. supra* note 4, at 9–10, 176, 210, 255, 270. On the absence of attention to the general survey of social directions, *cf.* Barnard, *The Functions of the Executive* (Cambridge, 1947), pp. 3–4; Chandler, *Henry Varnum Poor, Philosopher of Management*, in Miller, ed., *op. cit. supra* note 12, at 254, 265, 282–285; Dewey, *The Public and Its Problems* (2d ed. Chicago, 1946), pp. 159–184; Millett, *The Process and Organization of Government Planning* (New York, 1947), pp. 6–7, 92.

14. Blum and Kalven, *The Uneasy Case for Progressive Taxation* (Chicago, 1953), pp. 70–71; 3 Dorfman, *op. cit. supra* note 4, at 7–9, 256; Paul, *Taxation in the United States* (Boston, 1954), pp. 27, 30–31, 63, 90, 92, 93; Schumpeter, *op. cit. supra* note 7, at 769, 888, 945–946. There was some advocacy of the progressive income tax as a device to affect capital concentration, however. 3 Dorfman, *loc. cit. supra*, pp. 126, 218; Paul, *loc. cit. supra*, pp. 36, 88–89. On the cumulative force of events, *cf.* Jordy, *Henry Adams: Scientific Historian* (New Haven, 1952), pp. 98, 113, 133, 142–144, 213.

15. See the quotation and discussion in Lynch, *The Concentration of Economic Power* (New York, 1946), p. 9, note 3. On the considerable congruence between popular attitudes and those of the new entrepreneurs, see Cochran, *Role and Sanction in American Entrepreneurial History*, in Cole, ed., *Change and the Entrepreneur* (Cambridge, 1949), pp. 160, 161, 163, 170–171. The economists' search for determinist economic doctrine and their developing interest in social control at the turn of the century are discussed by Keilhau, *Principles of Private and Public Planning* (New York, 1952), p. 20, and Schumpeter, *op. cit. supra* note 7, at 945.

16. The quoted description of the immigrant societies is Handlin's, in *The Uprooted* (Boston, 1951), p. 177; on the development of association generally in the nineteenth-century United States, see Bogart, *Economic History of the American People* (2d ed. New York, 1938), pp. 593–594, 598; Smith, *A Dangerous Freedom* (Philadelphia, 1954), Chs. IX–XII; Williams, *American Society* (New York, 1951), pp. 466–472.

17. Linton, *The Cultural Background of Personality* (New York, 1945) pp. 11–12. For the quotation from Calhoun, see Ch. II of these essays, note 10. *Cf.* Griffith, *The Impasse of Democracy* (New York, 1939), pp. 32, 67, 114; MacIver, *Society* (New York, 1937), pp. 244–245, 251, 257 ff., 313.

18. The rights of association and assembly were established in our tradition

before they received formal constitutional acknowledgment. See *United States* v. *Cruikshank*, 92 U.S. 542, 551 (1875); Jarrett and Mund, *The Right of Assembly*, 9 N.Y.U.L.Q. Rev. 1, 12, 16–18 (1931). Reservation of the state's right to limit associations which might challenge the law's legitimate monopoly of force only underlined our general expectation that group action would ordinarily enjoy the law's support and protection. See *Presser* v. *Illinois*, 116 U.S. 252, 267 (1886); *New York* ex rel. *Bryant* v. *Zimmerman*, 278 U.S. 63, 72 (1928). *Cf.* Freund, *Administrative Powers over Persons and Property* (Chicago, 1928), pp. 68–69, 440–441; Dodd, *Dogma and Practice in the Law of Associations*, 42 Harv. L. Rev. 977, 985 (1929).

19. On the Illinois anarchist episode, see *Spies* v. *People*, 122 Ill. 1, 12 N.W. 865 (1887), and David, *History of the Haymarket Affair* (New York, 1936), Ch. XIV; compare, on the general nineteenth-century rejection of guilt by association, Chafee, *Free Speech in the United States* (Cambridge, 1942), pp. 101, 474, and *DeJonge* v. *Oregon*, 299 U.S. 353, 362–365 (1937), and especially its invocation of the Cruikshank opinion, at 364. Riot cases are noted in Hurst, *Treason in the United States*, 58 Harv. L. Rev. 806, 852–853 (1945). Thomas Beer has vividly depicted the atmosphere of the 1896 election, in *The Mauve Decade* (New York, 1926), pp. 85–88, and *Hanna* (New York, 1929), pp. 151–164. "Government by injunction" is discussed in Frankfurter and Greene, *The Labor Injunction* (New York, 1930), Ch. I, especially pp. 1, 6–10, 15–24; and see Dodd, *From Maximum Wages to Minimum Wages: Six Centuries of Regulation of Employment Contracts*, 43 Col. L. Rev. 643, 662–663 (1943). Legal doctrine recognizing the semiautonomous status of private associations, and the extent of power delegated to them, is set forth in Dodd, *op. cit. supra* note 18, at 984–985, 996; Chafee, *The Internal Affairs of Associations Not for Profit*, 43 Harv. L. Rev. 993, 996, 1010, 1016–1017, 1019, 1021–1027 (1930); Jaffe, *Law Making by Private Groups*, 51 *id.* 201, 219, 228–230, 231–233 (1937); Note, 35 *id.* 332 (1922).

20. 94 U.S. 113, 132 (1876).

21. Barnes, *The Economics of Public Utility Regulation* (New York, 1947), pp. 25, 27, 31–32, 35–36, 40; *cf.* note 1 *supra*.

22. Merk, *Economic History of Wisconsin during the Civil War Decade* (Madison, 1916), pp. 326, 329–330; see, *e.g.*, Wis. L. 1867, Memorial No. 11, Feb. 27, 1867; L. 1871, Memorial No. 15, Feb. 21, 1871; L. 1872, Jt. Res. No. 3, Feb. 14, 1872; L. 1875, Memorial No. 3, Feb. 17, 1875; *cf.* 33rd Wis. Legis., J. Sen., Jan. 15, 1880, pp. 11–12, and *id.*, J. Ass., Jan. 15, 1880, p. 14; Message of Gov. R. M. LaFollette, 47th Wis. Legis., J. Ass., Jan. 12, 1905, p. 19, at 62–63.

23. Barnes, *op. cit. supra* note 21, at 168–169; Radin, *op. cit. supra* note 5, at 581; Wherry, *Public Utilities—Progression or Retrogression?* 2 LAW, A *Century of Progress, 1835–1935*, 81, 97 (New York, 1937); on railroad consolidations in Wisconsin, see Merk, *op. cit. supra* note 22, Ch. XI; Hunt, *Law and Early Wisconsin Railroads* (Unpublished S.J.D. Thesis, on deposit in Law Library, University of Wisconsin, Madison, 1952), pp. 159–165, 310–311.

24. Compare Toynbee's comments on the trend toward "etherealization" in "mature" civilizations and the accompanying transfer of energy from lower

to higher spheres of being. 3 *A Study of History* 182 (London, 1934). Of similar import is the view of culture as a conversion of energy into institutions, in Coon, *The Story of Man* (New York, 1954), pp. 64, 114, 261, 423–424. See *German Alliance Insurance Co.* v. *Kansas*, 233 U.S. 389, 406, 411, 414 (1914); *Nebbia* v. *New York*, 291 U.S. 502, 537 (1934). Generally, on the contemporary growth of interest in social structure and process, see Commager, *op. cit. supra* note 4, at 199–220.

25. See Freund, *op. cit. supra* note 5, at 70–71; *cf.* Dicey, *Law and Public Opinion in England During the 19th Century* (London, 1914), pp. 364–370. In *Attorney General* v. *Railway Companies*, 35 Wis. 425 (1874), the action rested on the rate policy declared by a state statute, but the substance of the regulatory effort as Ryan would have shaped it would have been through exercise of the court's equity powers.

26. See Taft, J., in *United States* v. *Addyston Pipe & Steel Co.*, 85 Fed. 271, 282–283 (C.C.A. 6th. 1898); Handler, *A Study of the Construction and Enforcement of the Federal Anti-Trust Laws*, TNEC Monograph No. 38 (Washington, D.C., 1941), p. 4; Peppin, *Price-Fixing Agreements Under the Sherman Anti-Trust Law*, 28 Calif. L. Rev. 297, 350 (1940).

27. The Sherman Act is 26 Stat. 209. *Cf.* Hughes, C.J., in *Appalachian Coals, Inc.* v. *United States*, 288 U.S. 344, 359–360 (1933).

28. See *United States* v. *E.C. Knight Co.*, 156 U.S. 1 (1895); *Northern Securities Co.* v. *United States*, 193 U.S. 197 (1904); on the Industrial Commission of 1898, Lynch, *op. cit. supra* note 15, at 354, 371, 375, 387–388; on the executive initiative to seek a change in the Knight case doctrine, Theodore Roosevelt, *Autobiography* (New York, 1925), pp. 428–430, and Cummings and McFarland, *Federal Justice* (New York, 1937), pp. 328–331; on Roosevelt's general policy position, Blum, *The Republican Roosevelt* (Cambridge, 1954), pp. 27, 33, 35, 56–58, 74–75, 82, 86–105, 108–124; on the Bureau of Corporations, Stocking and Watkins, *op. cit. supra* note 1, at 35, 353, n. 23.

29. Labor attitudes are discussed by Perlman, *A Theory of the Labor Movement* (New York, 1928), pp. 157, 159–162, 163, 165, 167–168, 173, 187, 197–200; Dulles, *op. cit. supra* note 3, at 115, 126–127, 150, 153. Note the significance of the strong criticisms from conservative sources of the bringing of a "treason" prosecution against leaders of the Homestead strikers. See Hurst, *op. cit. supra* note 19, at 822–825. Handlin, *op. cit. supra* note 16, Ch. VIII, discusses the immigrant in metropolitan politics; *cf.* Blum, *op. cit. supra* note 28, at 64–65. The Jeffersonian conservatism of the late-century agrarian revolt may be seen in the analyses in McConnell, *op. cit. supra* note 3, at 3–9, and in Taylor, *op. cit. supra* note 3, at 162, 175, 305; on the Populists, see Taylor, pp. 230, 300, 305. The Declaration of Purpose of the National Grange is quoted by McConnell, p. 6.

30. General trends in social legislation are noted in Freund, *op. cit. supra* note 5, at 19, 85–86 (liquor), 20–22, 83 (health), 27–29 (hours of women), 70–71 (common law policy limits), 110 (industrial accident), 123–128, 271–272 (wage payment); and in Fabricant, *The Trend of Government Activity in the United States Since 1900* (New York, 1952), pp. 4–7, 61, 67, 73, 75–77, 78, 82–83, 140–141, 145; *cf.* Galloway and Kilpatrick, *Government Expendi-*

tures, in Dewhurst and Associates, *America's Needs and Resources* (New York, 1947), pp. 459, 468–469, 471, 473, 475. Law and public health are discussed by Alsburg, *Food and Drug Regulation,* 6 Encyc. Soc. Sci. 297 (New York, 1931); Winslow, *Public Health,* 12 *id.* 647 (New York, 1934); Goldmark, *Impatient Crusader* (Brandeis, ed. Urbana, 1953), p. 67; Regier, *The Struggle for Federal Food and Drugs Legislation,* 1 Law & Contemp. Prob. 3 (1933); Schlesinger, *op. cit. supra* note 1, at 244–246; Price, *Government and Science* (New York, 1954), pp. 9–10. On labor legislation, see Dodd, *op. cit. supra* note 19, at 658, 662–666; Kapp, *op. cit. supra* note 7, Ch. IV. The limitations of common law protection to the consumer are discussed in Handler, *False and Misleading Advertising,* 39 Yale L.J. 22 (1929); credit regulation, by Gallert, Hilborn and May, *Small-Loans Legislation* (New York, 1932), pp. 15, 18–26, and Chs. III, IV, also Nugent, *The Loan-Shark Problem,* 8 Law & Contemp. Prob. 3 (1941); insurance regulation, by Patterson, *The Insurance Commissioner in the United States* (Cambridge, 1927), pp. 520–537, and *Insurance, Law and Regulation,* 8 Enc. Soc. Sci. 106 (New York, 1932); see Vance, *Law of Insurance* (3rd ed. St. Paul, 1951), pp. 59–60.

31. Message of Jan. 10, 1862, 15th Wis. Legis., J. Sen., pp. 12–32, at 27–28. Typical expressions of confidence in the inexhaustible store of natural wealth are contained in Communication of Hon. Alfred Brunson, 4th Wis. Terr. Legis., 2d Sess., J.H.R., App., at 35; Ann. Rept. & Coll. of State Hist. Soc., 10th Wis. Legis. (1857), J. Ass., App., at 444; Report, (Assembly) Committee on Incorporation *re* Bill 9S, March 12, 1866, 19th Wis. Legis., J. Ass., p. 454; Report, Select Committee *re* St. Croix Land Grant, March 7, 1873, 26th Wis. Legis., J. Ass., pp. 705–710, at 705. Compare, generally, Pinchot, *Breaking New Ground* (New York, 1947), pp. 23–28.

32. Report of (Assembly) Select Committee *re* Bill 191A, Feb. 13, 1867, 20th Wis. Legis., J. Ass., pp. 283–286, at 283, 285.

33. The act authorizing the commission of inquiry was Wis. L. 1867, Ch. 36. The commission report was published as a pamphlet, Madison, 1867; see Report (Senate) Committee on Agriculture, Feb. 24, 1869, 22d Wis. Legis., J. Sen., p. 387, recommending against a second printing of the 1867 commission report as an unnecessary expense. The farm tree belt act was Wis. L. 1868, Ch. 102, am'd, L. 1876, Ch. 258, repealed upon creation of a state board of forestry, L. 1905, Ch. 264. In 1872 the Assembly defeated a bill to establish a state superintendent of forestry and provide for the cultivation of farm and forest trees. See 29th Wis. Legis., J. Ass. (1872), pp. 258, 351, 536, 586. Wis. L. 1897, Ch. 229, provided for a forest policy commission. Legislation following the recommendations of this commission included Wis. L. 1903, Ch. 450, and L. 1905, Ch. 264. See *State ex rel. Owen v. Donald,* 160 Wis. 21, 151 N.W. 331 (1915). *Cf.* First Annual Report, Wisconsin Regional Planning Committee (Madison, 1934), p. 221. Compare the comments on the similar pattern of development in national forest policy, in Gulick, *American Forest Policy* (New York, 1951), pp. 19–25; Pinchot, *op. cit. supra* note 31, at 79–86, 105–113, 120–122, 243–262.

34. Roosevelt, *op. cit. supra* note 28, at 79, 289; see Hofstadter, *The American Political Tradition* (New York, 1948), pp. 214–218.

35. *Cf.* Schlesinger, *op. cit. supra* note 1, at 104–105, 133–134, 244–246. But public health regulation lagged well into the twentieth century in smaller urban areas. See Lynd and Lynd, *Middletown* (New York, 1929), pp. 448–452, 456–457.

36. *Cf.* Alexander, *Our Age of Unreason* (Philadelphia, 1942), pp. 25, 134–137, 313–314; Cameron, *The Psychology of Behavior Disorders* (Boston, 1947), pp. 3–7, 581–584; Kardiner, *The Psychological Frontiers of Society* (New York, 1945), pp. 416, 442; Warner, Havighurst, and Loeb, *Who Shall Be Educated?* (New York, 1944), pp. 149, 157, 163.

37. The principal evidence of the growth of the matter-of-fact approach to public policy making is in the history of government budgets. See, *e.g.*, Fabricant, *op. cit. supra* note 30, at 148, 149, 153–154. A pointed contemporary appeal for social engineering over moralizing was that of Henry Demarest Lloyd, in *Wealth Against Commonwealth* (New York, 1894), p. 358. Compare the translation of William James into jurisprudence through Holmes, notably in the latter's "bad man's definition" of law, set out in *The Path of the Law*, in *Collected Legal Papers* (New York, 1920), p. 170. On the use of law to mobilize diffuse political force, *cf.* Final Report of the Attorney General's Committee on Administrative Procedure (Washington, D.C., 1941), pp. 13, 14, 15–17, 19, 20; Report of Commissioner Robert M. Benjamin, Administrative Adjudication in the State of New York (Albany, 1942), pp. 13, 22, 297–299. The wider spreading of practical popular power in politics is discussed in 1 LaFollette, *Robert M. LaFollette* 103, 119, 143, 160 (New York, 1953); *cf.* Gross, *The Legislative Struggle* (New York, 1953), pp. 137–158; Note, 45 Harv. L. Rev. 1241 (1932). The decision which launched the new significance of the presumption of constitutionality was *Powell* v. *Pennsylvania*, 127 U.S. 678 (1888); *cf.* Notes, 31 Col. L. Rev. 1136 (1931), and 36 *id.* 283 (1936); on the implications for the leeway thus accorded pressure groups, see *Daniel* v. *Family Security Life Insurance Co.*, 336 U.S. 220, 224 (1949). *Powell* v. *Pennsylvania* represented the eventual compromise between the drastically limited scope of judicial review under Waite's majority opinion and the extremely broad extent of the power indicated in Field's dissent in the same case; by mid–twentieth century the compromise worked out much closer to Waite than to Field. *Cf. The Sinking Fund Cases*, 99 U.S. 700 (1878). See, generally, Nelles, Book Review, 40 Yale L.J. 998, 999, 1000 (1931).

38. Kapp, *op. cit. supra* note 7, at 9, 11, 14, 24, 247, 254, 257, discusses the acknowledgment of the existence of social costs, implied in government budgets and regulations. Characteristic end-of-century recognition of the need to distinguish between social capital and social income will be found in 7th Bienn. Rept., Wis. Bureau of Labor, Census and Industrial Statistics, Sept. 30, 1896, 43rd Wis. Legis., 2 Public Documents, at 145; and in Report of Wisconsin Forestry Commission (1898), 44th Wis. Legis., 2 Public Documents, at 5–6, 10, 22. On the concealed subsidy involved in the absence of desirable social regulations, *cf. Reagan* v. *Farmers' Loan and Trust Co.*, 154 U.S. 362, 412 (1894); *Covington and Lexington Turnpike Road Co.* v. *Sandford*, 164 U.S. 578, 596–597 (1896); *Holden* v. *Hardy*, 169 U.S. 366, 392–397 (1898); and see Blum, *op. cit. supra* note 28, at 74–75; Webb, *The Great Plains* (New York, 1931), pp.

233, 238, 241, 393, 411, 430. The reassessment of the comparative desirability of placing loss on injured individuals or on serviced groups is discussed in Ehrenzweig, *Negligence Without Fault* (Berkeley and Los Angeles, 1951), pp. 10, 14, 40, 86; Gardner, *Insurance Against Tort Liability*, 15 Law & Contemp. Prob. 455, 462 (1950); Goldmark, *op. cit. supra* note 30, at 38, 95, and Chs. V, VII; Green, *The Individual's Protection under Negligence Law: Risk Sharing*, 47 N.W. Univ. L. Rev. 751, 753, 755, 760 (1953); Douglas, *Vicarious Liability and Administration of Risk*, 38 Yale L.J. 584 (1929); James, *Accident Liability Reconsidered: The Impact of Liability Insurance*, 57 *id.* 549 (1948), and *Social Insurance and Tort Liability: The Problem of Alternative Remedies*, 27 N.Y.U.L.Q. Rev. 537 (1954); and *Assumption of Risk*, 61 Yale L.J. 141, 153–157, 168–169 (1952).

39. The quotation is from Mr. Justice Frankfurter's Foreword to Goldmark, *op. cit. supra* note 30, at vi, vii. On the increase in the use of data collection and analysis as means of the law's impact on society, see Holmes, *op. cit. supra* note 37, at 196, and *Speeches* (Boston, 1918), pp. 82, 85–86; Gaus and Wolcott, *Public Administration and the United States Department of Agriculture* (Chicago, 1940), pp. 5, 6; 2 Kirkland, *Men, Cities and Transportation* 238–240, 332–335 (2 vols. Cambridge, 1952); Price, *op. cit. supra* note 30, at 4, 9–10, 20–27, 34–39, 62–63, 108, 158; *cf.* Freund, *op. cit. supra* note 5, at 249–260; Chandler, *op. cit. supra* note 13, at 276–281; Cross, *The People's Right to Know* (New York, 1953), pp. 6, 14–18, 25–29, 51, 55.

INDEX